The Bristol Avon
Fish, Freshwater Life and Fishing

D. E. Tucker

Millstream Books

First published 1987

Millstream Books
7 Orange Grove
Bath BA1 1LP

This book is set in Baskerville
Typeset by Character Graphics, Taunton
Cover printed by The Matthews Wright Press, Chard

ISBN 0948975083

Cover illustrations:
Front cover – the Bristol Avon below Avoncliff Aqueduct
Back cover – family fishing at Freshford

Printed in Great Britain by A. Wheaton & Co. Ltd., Exeter

Contents

In memory of
TOMMY DYER
(1891-1956)
Bristolian, sailor,
naturalist, angler and
Head Water Bailiff Emeritus

Author's Preface

This is a book not only for anglers but also for naturalists, teachers, walkers and all who enjoy the countryside. Books about the Avon are few. Sixty years have passed since Ernest Walls wrote a delightful book entitled *The Bristol Avon*, an antiquary's account of his wanderings down-river from Tetbury to Avonmouth, with reference to political history and literary connections. Mine is a very different book, concerned with what happens in the living world beneath the surface: not only what fish are there and what they look like but why they are there, what they feed on and what feeds on them. The theme for angler and naturalist alike is: only connect! Examples quoted are mostly local to the Bristol Avon catchment, but the principles they exemplify may be equally true of other parts of lowland Britain and give food for thought to a wider public.

Both in earning my living as Pollution Prevention & Fisheries Officer for the Bristol Avon River Board and its successor the River Authority, and in writing this book in retirement, I have been constantly aware that most of what I know and have been able to use and communicate has come from the patient work of others. Now dead or still living, they are too numerous to recall and name, but I do acknowledge their help and so far as it is possible thank them sincerely. Specifically my thanks are extended to the Wessex Water Authority and the staff of the Bristol Avon Division for allowing me to use their records to keep my information up to date.

Woolley Mill, Bath.   D. E. TUCKER

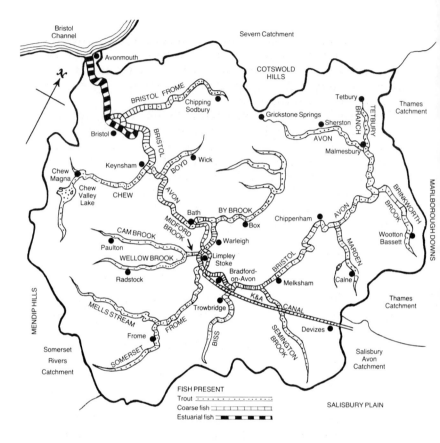

Fig. 1 Sketch-map of the Bristol Avon catchment area, showing principal rivers, the Kennet & Avon Canal and types of fish present.

1. The River

The Bristol Avon is so called to distinguish it from the Salisbury or Hampshire Avon, the Stratford or Warwickshire Avon, the Gloucestershire or Little Avon and several others, the name 'Avon' being derived from a Celtic word meaning no more than 'river'.

Our river rises in the Cotswold Hills above Sherston and flows clockwise through pastoral countryside and the towns of Malmesbury, Chippenham, Melksham, Bradford-on-Avon, Bath, Keynsham and finally Bristol, where it becomes a ten-mile-long estuary that joins the Severn estuary at Avonmouth. The catchment area measures 857 square miles (2217 square kilometres), and the median river flow at Bath, in the centre of the area, is about 240 million gallons per day (12.6 cubic metres per second).

The course of the river is an old one, originally cut on land surfaces that have long since been planed down. River captures have intervened, so stretches that once flowed east now flow south and finally west: a map of the river suggests a reaping hook. As a result, although the distance by river from source to mouth is 88 miles (142 km), as a crow flies it is only 17 miles (27.3 km).

The principal tributaries of the Avon (and their townships) are the Tetbury branch, the Brinkworth Brook (Wootton Bassett), the River Marden (Calne), the Semington Brook (Devizes), the River Biss (Trowbridge), the Somerset Frome (Frome), the Midford Brook (fed by the Wellow Brook from Midsomer Norton and the Cam Brook from Paulton), the By Brook or Weaver (Box), the River Boyd (Wick), the River Chew (Chew Magna) and the Bristol Frome (Chipping Sodbury). The Kennet & Avon Canal enters the catchment area near Devizes and joins the Avon at Bath after 22 miles (35.4 km).

The character of a river is largely dependent on local geology. Our river basin is rimmed by low hills: in the south-west the Mendips, of carboniferous limestone; in the north the Cotswolds, of Jurassic limestone; and in the east and south the Marlborough Downs and scarp of Salisbury Plain, of chalk. While much of the basin presents an appearance of green fields and scattered woodland, its floor consists of soft sedimentary rocks, mostly impervious clays: keuper marl, lias, fullers' earth, Oxford and Kimmeridge clays and gault. In the event of heavy rainfall there is consequently rapid run-off, the tributaries and the Avon itself becoming swollen, deep and forceful. Such rivers are called 'flashy'. At Bath, for instance, the ratio of maximum known flood flow to mean river flow is 18.7 to 1. This contrasts with, say, the Salisbury Avon at Ringwood, in a semi-permeable chalk catchment, where the ratio is only 5.6 to 1.

Swollen waters cut deep channels in soft rocks, so our brooks and rivers now flow in the bottoms of narrow trenches. Erosion is still going on, so there is often fine clay in suspension, giving the water a cloudy appearance and reducing penetration of sunlight. Much of the fresh-water Avon and its tributaries is backed up by old milling weirs, however, which serve to retain water in the deeply cut channels even when flow is small. Waters ponded behind the weirs go through cycles: slow and placid in dry weather, fast and turbulent in wet. Following the turbulence is a stage when there is still fine silt and clay in suspension but speed is decreasing, so suspended particles settle out. Eventually the water becomes very clear, but when the next spate happens, speed and turbulence increase, so the sediments and anything they hold come back into suspension. This is unfortunate for many of the small plants and invertebrate animals that form a production line contributing to the food of fish: in wet weather they scour away and at least some are carried out to sea.

Besides instability of habitat, lack of light is detrimental to production. The growth of algae and fine water weeds that can use daylight to produce food material is restricted where cloudiness, deep water, a steep bank or bankside vegetation reduces the access of light.

The Bristol Avon with its heavy subsoils may thus be at a disadvantage in the production of freshwater fish by comparison with the Salisbury Avon, but like that river its spring waters have percolated through strata of chalk or limestone, so are alkaline and rich in basic mineral elements necessary for the growth of plants and animals. Both Avons have a distinct advantage over moorland streams and rivers from catchments of hard rock such as are found farther west and in parts of Wales and Scotland. Our invertebrates – lowly members of the animal kingdom that are too primitive to have the benefit of backbones – are of various kinds and plentiful, so it is not surprising to find that fish, which are partly dependent on them for food, are of fair sizes and good numbers in our Avon, and give consistent fishing.

The Sherston and Tetbury branches hold trout, minnows, gudgeon and occasional grayling, but in their slacker stretches behind weirs they are infiltrated by roach, chub, dace, eels, perch, bleak and tench, as well as predatory pike, that have worked their way up from slower water downstream.

From Malmesbury down to Great Somerford all the above species are found, plus some barbel. Proceeding down-river to Bath, the species are similar with the addition of bream. As the river flattens out, the carp family tends to increase in numbers while trout and especially grayling become less evident. Estimates of fish in water are notoriously imprecise and subjective, and local fluctuations can be expected, but a diminishing order of frequency might read: roach, bream, chub, gudgeon, eel, pike, minnow, dace, bleak, tench, trout, perch, barbel, carp, with a few rudd and grayling.

From Bath, through Saltford and Keynsham to Netham, grayling are absent, trout are comparatively scarce, rudd and barbel are few, but flounders are sometimes to be found between Keynsham and Netham. Below Netham Dam the river becomes a tidal estuary. More is said of this in Chapters 2 and 6.

Of the smaller fishes not mentioned above, sticklebacks may be observed in shallow water wherever there are other fish; bullheads (miller's thumbs) are widespread wherever water flows strongly over a stony bottom; stone loach are encountered in most of the hill streams, and brook lampreys may be found in favourable locations where the hill streams flatten out to lowland river, as in the Avon near Great Somerford and the Chew near Chewton Keynsham.

In the Avon tributaries the upper stretches hold small trout, minnows, gudgeon and eels, while the lower stretches are similar to the Avon. As might be expected, the Kennet & Avon Canal holds no trout or grayling but is well stocked with 'coarse' fish, including perch and large pike. A list of other fishable waters associated with the Avon, and the kinds of fish they hold, is given in Appendix 2.

9

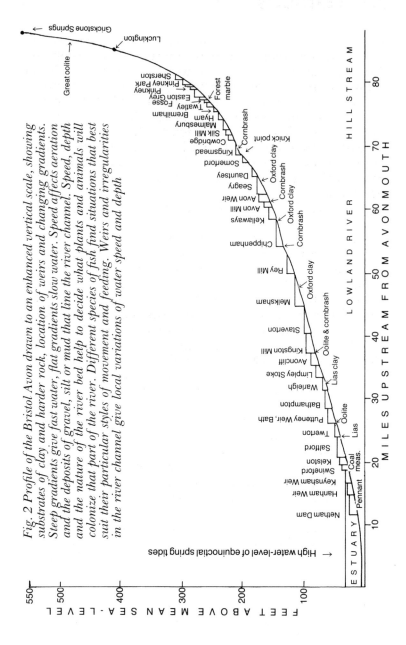

Fig. 2 Profile of the Bristol Avon drawn to an enhanced vertical scale, showing substrates of clay and harder rock, location of weirs and changing gradients. Steep gradients give fast water, flat gradients slow water. Speed affects aeration and the deposits of gravel, silt or mud that line the river channel. Speed, depth and the nature of the river bed help to decide what plants and animals will colonize that part of the river. Different species of fish find situations that best suit their particular styles of movement and feeding. Weirs and irregularities in the river channel give local variations of water speed and depth

10

2. Habitats

The Bristol Avon and its tributaries fall naturally into three habitat zones, in each of which the living-conditions for water creatures are somewhat different. These are (a) the comparatively steep and fast-running hill streams, (b) the slow-moving lowland river and (c) the narrow estuary, scoured twice daily by wide-ranging tides. Although weirs have obscured the exact places where one passes to another, the zones show up clearly on a longitudinal section of the Avon by their gradients, and each has a characteristic flora and fauna.

(a) A part of the Avon that may typically be regarded as a hill stream is the Sherston branch, which in 17 miles (27.3 km) drops down 210 feet (64 m) through Malmesbury to Great Somerford, where the lowland section of river may be said to start: an overall gradient of 1 in 427. The Tetbury branch of the Avon and much of the tributaries are hill streams with similar gradients giving water speeds that minimize the deposit of clay and ensure good oxygenation. In many ways they are like the chalk streams of Hampshire, but they are cut deeply and their stony bottoms are in places lightly overlaid with mud. Filamentous green algae, willow moss and stream crowfoot (*Ranunculus pseudo-fluitans*) flourish in our hill streams and shelter a diverse and plentiful fauna, notably caddis and mayfly larvae, water beetles, freshwater shrimps and operculate snails. Hill streams are ideal waters for trout, grayling, minnows, stone loach and bullheads.

(b) The lowland Avon falls from 190 feet (58 metres) above sea-level, at Great Somerford, to 20 feet (6.1 m) at Netham Dam, Bristol, in a distance of 57 miles (92 km), an apparent gradient of 1 in 1770, but in fact a series of long basins, for there are 23 mill weirs at mean intervals of 2½ miles (4 km). Below each weir the river has scoured a deep pool where the water is always well aerated but slow to move on. Such pools are prestige habitats for specimen fish. The lowest stretches of the larger tributaries are lowland river with similar gradients and weir pools.

Immediately downstream of each weir pool is a shoal of

11

gravel covered by shallow fast-moving water, and this is succeeded by irregular pools, silt banks and rapids until the water progressively deepens and slows on approaching the next weir. Immediately upstream of the weir the water will be deep, probably of the order of 10 feet (3 m).

The lowland zone, with its accompanying bottom, banks, structures, tree roots and other vegetation, presents a diversity of habitats colonized by a wide range of plants and animals. Typical riverside trees are alders, crack willows (*Salix fragilis*) and the bushy grey sallow (*Salix atrocinerea*). Shoals in the river are colonized by rushes, and deep water by yellow water-lilies, commonly known as 'brandy-bottles' because of their flask-shaped fruits that smell of alcohol; a bed of water-lilies, trap for anglers' tackle, is derisively called a 'cabbage patch'. Varying depths and speeds of river allow at least eight distinct species of pondweed (*Potamogeton*) to flourish here. In places the riverside is rich in emergent plants that like to enjoy the protection of the banks but keep their roots in water (common reed, the branched and unbranched bur-reeds, reedmace, bulrush, giant sweetgrass, flowering rush) and a multitude of marsh flowers that tolerate both flooding in winter and drying-out at the roots in summer. The emergent plants are especially important for the production of aquatic insect larvae, as they provide somewhere to lay eggs, they harbour larvae in and among their roots, and they are skyward ladders when the debutant insects are ready to try their wings.

The lowland river is ideal water for roach, but the variety of depths and speeds offers niches for other members of the carp family as well as for larger trout that drop down from the hill streams, and for predatory and scavenging species.

(c) The lowest zone is the estuary, where waters oscillate twice daily from a narrow stream of fresh river water to a turbid flood of half-dilute sea water – and back again. A century of gross pollution in the estuary is now practically at an end, but this is still a difficult environment for anything to live in, whether plant or animal. Brackish-water species of green algae known as *Enteromorpha* are able to grow attached to hard surfaces, and channel-wrack and flat-wrack find a precarious hold on piers at the Avonmouth end of the estuary. Ragworms and the little operculate snails called Jenkins' spire-shells are able to live happily in the estuarine mud. But, apart from the ubiquitous sticklebacks that live in brackish rhines behind sea walls, and sea-going eels that drop down-river in autumn, any fish found here are likely to have been carried in from the Bristol Channel by flux of the tide. Flounders, bass, thin-lipped grey mullet and twaite shad come into the Avon estuary from the Severn; occasional dabs, small soles, small cod, whiting, conger, sprats, dogfish and thornback rays may wander there from the Somerset and North Devon coast. The presence of salmon and sea trout is discussed later, in the chapter on the salmon family.

Additionally there are three artificial habitat zones: (*d*) the Kennet & Avon Canal, constructed 1796-1810, once an actively flowing part of the river system but now suffering from long-standing neglect; (*e*) the Bristol Floating Harbour and Feeder Canal, constructed 1804-09, and until 1977 in constant use by commercial shipping but now given over to recreational use; and (*f*) ornamental lakes and reservoirs, most of them formed by damming hill streams. These last three habitat zones have in common a fertile water but minimal water speed. Not surprisingly they are 'eutrophic', a condition (discussed at length in the next chapter) that manifests itself by intermittent shortage of oxygen.

(*d*) The Kennet & Avon Canal is no longer filled to its designed water-levels, and parts of it from time to time have had to be drained out because of leaks on slipping hillsides. Praiseworthy efforts to restore the Canal as a through waterway for boats have been made by the Kennet & Avon Canal Trust in collaboration with British Waterways Board and other statutory and voluntary bodies, but its maintenance is still problematical. Much of the water surface is covered by lesser duckweed and (apparently in diminishing quantity) by the water fern, *Azolla filiculoides*; these exclude light below the surface and thus aggravate the summertime shortage of oxygen. A rich flora of swamp and marsh plants has encroached on the channel and banks. Fishing is nevertheless popular, for carp, tench, roach, common bream and gudgeon are able to withstand the eutrophic conditions, together with eels, pike and – in favourable places – perch and rudd.

The Kennet & Avon Canal has wider fluctuations of temperature than the flowing rivers. In the twenty-five years up to 1976 the highest known natural river-water temperature on the Avon was 78° Fahrenheit (25.5 ° Celsius), which was reached in several years in July, but the local still-water record was higher: 80° F (26.7° C) in the Kennet & Avon Canal at Bathampton on the 1st July 1952. These figures were both slightly exceeded in the exceptional conditions of 1976, a drought year. The Canal ices over earlier in hard winter weather than does the river (a rare occurrence) and remains at freezing-point for longer. In a cold springtime, canal water may not warm up sufficiently for the spawning requirements of some species of fish, notably at least 66° F (19° C) for tench and 68° F (20° C) for rudd. The result of such a non-event is a missing year-class for the species.

(e) Special considerations apply to the Bristol Floating Harbour and Feeder Canal, because they receive periodic influxes of salt water when spring tides are flowing in the estuary, while they are continuously topped up by fresh water from the Avon and the Bristol Frome, which reduces salt to a negligible level. The fish there are mostly freshwater colonists that can tolerate the salinity changes, though estuarine species might also be encountered. They include roach, dace, carp, tench, common bream, chub, stickleback, pike, perch, eel and flounder.

(f) Some of the ornamental lakes date back to the time of 'Capability' Brown, the 18th century landscape architect; a few are of even older, monastic origin. The reservoirs are more recent, the latest and largest being Chew Valley Lake, over 1½ miles wide and 2¼ miles long (2.4 by 3.6 km), constructed 1951-55. A noticeable sign of the ageing of a lake is the build-up of sedges and other swamp plants around its margins – the same emergent plants as are noted for hugging the banks of slow stretches of river.

The 'Capability' Brown lakes were once good trout waters but are no longer so; they are, however, suitable for the so-called coarse fish that have lower metabolic rates. Trout do thrive in Chew Valley Lake, both brownies and rainbows, because eutrophication is only incipient there and the vast surface area, exposed to wind action, helps to maintain dissolved oxygen at a sufficient level.

3.   Beneath the Surface

Fish happily swimming in water are visible evidence of life beneath the surface. The infra-structure of the fish world, however, is less obvious. Many questions may be asked. How, for instance, do fish obtain energy for moving about?

Energy

The energy that makes rivers flow comes from the sun, which warms the surface of the oceans, provides heat for evaporation and promotes winds to lift water vapour against the natural pull of gravity and precipitate it as rain on high land, whence it gathers into streams and gravitates down to sea-level. Only an insignificant part of the energy by which a fish moves, however, is derived from the energy of the surrounding water, which a fish uses by inclination of its paired fins like a glider in a thermal current of air. Fish propulsion is mainly accomplished by muscular energy, applied through undulations of the whole body. This energy is also derived from the sun, but in an indirect manner. Foodstuffs are first generated by photosynthesis; then, through a chain of lower organisms, eating and being eaten, the foodstuffs become part of the fish body, available to give back energy in a way comparable to fuel burning.

Photosynthesis

A connection between sunshine and the growth of crops has been taken for granted since the earliest days of mankind's activity as a cultivator. By the end of the 19th century it was recognized that various pigments in green plants, collectively called chlorophyll, as well as red and blue pigments in seaweeds, are responsible for assisting a natural process by which sunlight combines atmospheric carbon dioxide with water to produce sugars and other food substances. Oxygen is liberated as a by-product of the process, which used to be called carbon assimilation but is now usually known as photosynthesis. It was not until the middle of the 20th century, when radio-isotopes of carbon and

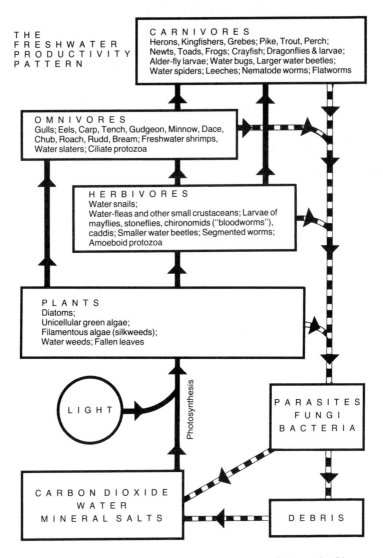

CARNIVORES
Herons, Kingfishers, Grebes; Pike, Trout, Perch;
Newts, Toads, Frogs; Crayfish; Dragonflies & larvae;
Alder-fly larvae; Water bugs, Larger water beetles;
Water spiders; Leeches; Nematode worms; Flatworms

OMNIVORES
Gulls; Eels, Carp, Tench, Gudgeon, Minnow, Dace,
Chub, Roach, Rudd, Bream; Freshwater shrimps,
Water slaters; Ciliate protozoa

HERBIVORES
Water snails;
Water-fleas and other small crustaceans; Larvae of
mayflies, stoneflies, chironomids ("bloodworms"),
caddis; Smaller water beetles; Segmented worms;
Amoeboid protozoa

PLANTS
Diatoms;
Unicellular green algae;
Filamentous algae (silkweeds);
Water weeds; Fallen leaves

LIGHT

Photosynthesis

**PARASITES
FUNGI
BACTERIA**

**CARBON DIOXIDE
WATER
MINERAL SALTS**

DEBRIS

*Fig. 3 The freshwater productivity pattern: some fish are herbivorous
(eating vegetation), some are carnivorous (eating other animals) and
some are omnivorous (eating both types of food); but all depend on the
production line that starts with photosynthesis, i.e. the build-up of simple
chemicals into vegetable material, a process driven by the energy of light
and made possible by plant pigments*

oxygen and new techniques of chromatography were used to trace and identify the molecules taking part, that photosynthesis was shown to be a complex series of recycling reactions.

The products of photosynthesis can include not only readily soluble carbohydrates such as sugars, and less soluble ones such as starches and cellulose, but also oils, fats, waxes and proteins. Supplementary chemical elements such as phosphorus, nitrogen and sulphur, that are essential to the build-up of such products, are obtainable in large quantities from the effluents that now enter rivers, as well as from natural sources such as minerals and atmospheric ammonia. The Bristol Avon is far more fertile in this respect than it was before, say, the Second World War. Photosynthesis takes place both in land plants and water plants, not least the microscopic ones such as diatoms and other unicellular algae. Tiny as they are, they are present in massive quantities. In May 1976, in response to the sunlight and warmth of the 1975-76 drought, diatoms in the Bristol Avon at Kellaways reached a peak of 20,300 per millilitre and unicellular green algae numbered 10,200 per ml.

Besides providing food for young fish and for many species of invertebrate animals, diatoms and other algae are especially useful in maintaining levels of dissolved oxygen in slow and still waters where there is little surface agitation to assist in the uptake of oxygen from the air. Plants with floating leaves, however, such as water-lilies and duckweed, are not good oxygenators; they produce their oxygen at the water surface, not deep down where it could be better utilized, and they cut off light from algae and other plants lower in the water.

Respiration

Using digested foodstuffs to produce energy is the reverse of photosynthesis and is known as respiration. Just as in burning a fuel such as coal or oil, respiration uses up oxygen. In plant and animal bodies, respiration takes place in stages that are activated and controlled by specific enzymes, which have to be manufactured as part of the process. Enzymes are sensitive to temperature; that is why a fish becomes sluggish and cannot digest at temperatures much above or below those to which it is accustomed.

Productivity

The general pattern of freshwater productivity is that daylight provides energy for the growth of vegetable material, some of it planktonic (i.e. free to drift about), some of it static. Herbivorous animals, whether fish or invertebrates, feed upon the vegetable material. Carnivores then feed upon the herbivores, but primary carnivores may in turn be eaten by secondary carnivores. There are also omni-

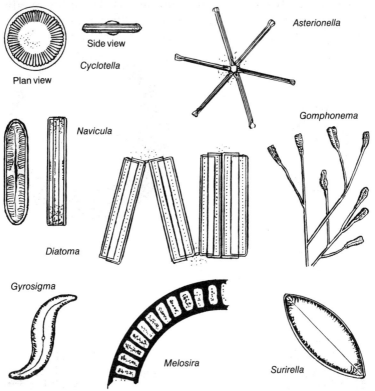

Fig. 4 Diatoms. These are microscopic single-celled plants formed as if by joining two parts in the manner of date-boxes or pill-boxes. Some are stalked, but many are anchored to plant stems or the water bottom only by strands of mucus, so they easily become detached. Their structure is of silica, not cellulose; their pigments are predominantly yellowish, and the products of their photosynthesis are oils, not sugars or starches. Diatoms are food for very young fish as well as for small invertebrate animals, which in turn become food for other aquatic animals

vores, which eat various proportions of vegetable and animal food, and may be eaten by carnivores; some may include dead or decaying material in their diets as well as living organisms. Parasites impose a small tax on productivity but yield little or nothing in return.

A single productivity chain rarely exceeds five links. A good example, common to the Bristol Avon and other temperate rivers, starts with the diatom *Navicula viridula*, which encrusts the river bed and any plants or other objects there. This is browsed on by swimming larvae of the mayfly *Baëtis rhodani* (a herbivore). The mayfly larvae are eaten by free-living larvae of the caddis fly *Rhyacophila dorsalis*

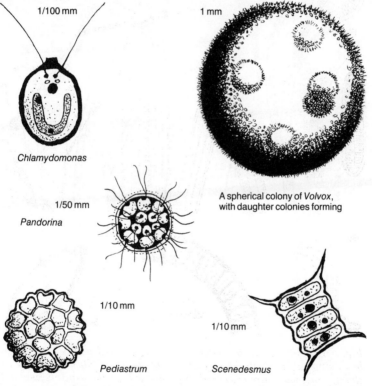

Fig. 5 Unicellular green algae. These vary greatly in size, so are food for a wide range of small fishes, particularly young fish in progressive stages of growth, as well as for water-fleas, other crustaceans and the smaller insect larvae that become food for fish and other freshwater animals

19

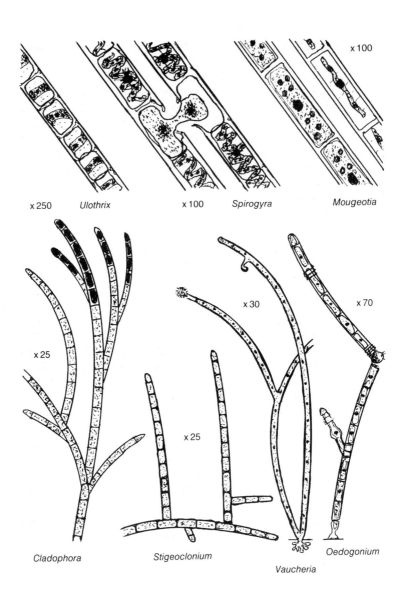

×100

×250   *Ulothrix*   ×100   *Spirogyra*   *Mougeotia*

×30

×70

×25

×25

Cladophora   *Stigeoclonium*   *Oedogonium*

Vaucheria

Fig. 6 Filamentous algae (silkweeds) grow attached to solid objects in the water but break away and drift. They are food for a wide range of invertebrate animals as well as for fish. They also provide shelter for small invertebrates and anchorage for diatoms

20

(primary carnivores). The caddis larvae are in turn eaten by dace (omnivores). And dace become prey for pike (secondary carnivores).

The individual organisms at the start of a productivity chain are highly numerous; those at the top end comparatively few. In terms of dry weight or of calories rather than numbers, each stage takes something of the order of 10 units of prey to produce 1 unit of predator, but the ratios can vary widely: estimates lie between 3.3 to 1 and 20 to 1.

The example is only one of many. *Navicula viridula* is browsed on by other species of invertebrate animals and is itself only one of many species of diatoms, not to mention the various green and other algae and other starting-points for food chains. The word 'chains' is indeed scarcely adequate: freshwater productivity is in fact a very dense web.

There is a saying 'Look after the pence and the pounds will look after themselves'. In freshwater terms, the small forms of life that are the primary producers are important. They need freedom from disturbance of the water bottom, freedom from pollution, and abundance of sunlight. It is significant that the sections of the Bristol Avon where the heaviest diatom and other algal counts have been made are devoid of overshadowing trees; so too are the places where the heaviest weights of fish have been caught.

If, in a mixed fishery such as the Bristol Avon, a management objective is to maximize weight of fish available for catching, then pike and other top carnivores can be seen as undesirable agents reducing that weight while themselves contributing only a fraction of what they take. The introduction of further predators such as the pike-perch or zander (*Stizostedion lucioperca*) could likewise be regarded as a dissipation of resources. Optimum production of fish in the Bristol Avon seems to lie with the omnivores, specifically the carp family, outstanding among which are roach and the common bream.

The Oxygen Balance

Whereas land animals find little difficulty in taking oxygen from the air, in order to breathe, water organisms have to use *dissolved* oxygen, which is always limited in supply. Air contains 23 per cent of oxygen by weight, 21

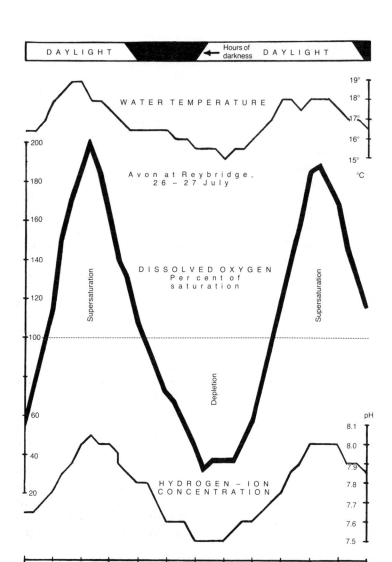

Fig. 7 Nightly depletion of dissolved oxygen. During hours of sunshine, carbon dioxide (carbonic acid gas) is converted into carbohydrates; alkalinity therefore rises (as indicated by pH values) and oxygen is produced as a by-product. In summer there is often supersaturation. During hours of darkness, however, respiration predominates and dissolved oxygen is progressively used up

per cent by volume, but water does not dissolve more than 14 parts of oxygen *per million* at normal atmospheric pressure. (The amount of dissolved oxygen in water can be expressed either as milligrams of dissolved oxygen per litre of water, usually called parts per million, or as a percentage of saturation *at the prevailing water temperature*. The latter is more meaningful in a biological situation, where what matters is availability rather than absolute quantity.)

Even plants breathe in the course of growing, though their respiration is obscured in daylight hours by photosynthesis going on simultaneously. Decaying plant and animal remains also consume oxygen, because they are fed upon by bacteria, which multiply and can go on respiring until all dissolved oxygen is used up. A similar thing happens if organically rich effluents such as silage liquor find their way into a watercourse. Although bacteria are individually microscopic, on such occasions colonies of the bacterium *Sphaerotilus natans* (usually called 'sewage fungus' but neither sewage nor a fungus) can often be detected as flocculent masses, like greyish cotton wool, clothing the water bottom and adjacent objects.

Dissolved oxygen is partly replenished by diffusion of air through the water surface, especially where the surface is broken up in rapids and waterfalls or by wind action, but nevertheless it fluctuates continually, increasing in daylight hours because of photosynthesis and decreasing in hours of darkness because of continuing respiration. Long sunny days in summer can lead to a state of supersaturation, that is more oxygen is produced by photosynthesis than can be dissolved, but in globules so small that surface tension holds them against upward flotation. When water is warm the respiration of plants and animals increases, so in hours of darkness all dissolved oxygen may be used up.

Eutrophication

When oxygen consumption has exceeded supply, fish come gasping to the surface, and unless the situation quickly improves they may die of suffocation. Lowland sections of the Bristol Avon that receive large flows of sewage-works effluent tend to be vulnerable, as are the Kennet & Avon Canal and 'Capability' Brown lakes, particularly in the hours before dawn during a heat wave. Fortunately the light of the rising sun usually saves the situation. Accumulation of plant and animal remains is a contributory factor in slow and static waters, for decay not only uses dissolved oxygen but it liberates mineral salts, which stimulate further plant growth. Waters that suffer like this are termed 'eutrophic', from a Greek word meaning 'nourished well'; unfortunately all is not well, for eutrophication is a sign of decline. It is not quite the same thing as stagnation, for stagnant waters are not necessarily eutrophic, and even moving rivers may become eutrophic. Rather, it is a chronic condition that shows itself by periodic oxygen shortage, especially in high summer (see Fig. 7).

Fast-moving fish such as trout and grayling are at special risk because they need at least 70 per cent of dissolved-oxygen saturation; lethargic fish such as carp and tench, however, can survive at no more than 10 per cent of saturation and may find eutrophic waters not only tolerable but

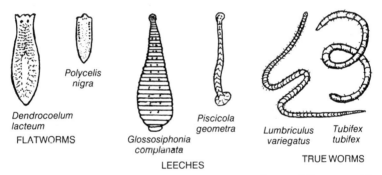

Fig. 8 Flatworms, leeches and true worms. Two classes of flatworms (the tapeworms and the flukes) are internal parasites of fish and other animals; a third class (the turbellarians) are free-living and carnivorous, eating small animals of all kinds, especially crustaceans and insects, usually by sucking off pieces of prey through a tubular mouth underneath the flat body.

Leeches are external parasites of fish and other animals. The body is made up of tapering segments, is flattened and has an adhesive sucker at each end.

True worms are also made up of segments but are round in section and have four bundles of minute bristles on each segment. Besides earthworms there are numerous freshwater and marine species, ingesting mud, diatoms and unicellular algae; they are an important item of food for fish

24

actually nourishing. Most aquatic animals are more or less sensitive to oxygen shortage; some (such as stonefly and mayfly larvae) more so than others, while 'bloodworms' (chironomid larvae with haemoglobin in their body-fluid) are able to utilize oxygen down to low levels.

OPERCULATE SNAILS

| Valve shell, *Valvata piscinalis* | Spire shell, *Potamopyrgus* (= *Hydrobia*) *jenkinsi* | *Bythinia tentaculata* | Freshwater winkle, *Viviparus* (= *Paludina*) *viviparus* |

PULMONATE SNAILS

| River limpet, *Ancylastrum* (= *Ancylus*) *fluviatile* | Bladder snail, *Physa* (= *Aplecta*) *fontinalis* | Wandering snail, *Limnaea peregra* | Ram's-horn snail, *Planorbis planorbis* |

BIVALVES

All about ⅔ size

Orb-shell, *Sphaerium corneum*   River pea-shell, *Pisidium amnicum*

Fig. 9 Molluscs. Water snails feed by rasping diatoms and algal slime from plants and other underwater objects; they become the food of carnivorous animals, including fish. Operculate snails can close the shell by means of an operculum or lid. They absorb dissolved oxygen through their thin shells and make use of it with the aid of gills, but can subsist only in clean, well-oxygenated water. Pulmonate snails, however, which are thought to have reverted from terrestrial ancestors, have no lid but come to the surface to trap air in a cavity under the mantle; they can survive in poorly oxygenated and eutrophic waters.

Freshwater mussels and cockles lie half-buried in the mud of slow and still waters, extracting dissolved oxygen from the water, together with small algal particles and water-fleas, by means of a siphon-and-filter system. Mussels are too large to figure in the diet of all but the biggest fish; but orb-shell and pea-shell cockles are much sought after by fish, their hard shells being digested by acid in the fishes' stomachs

25

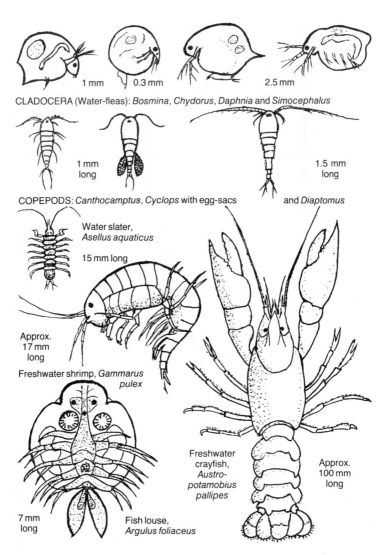

CLADOCERA (Water-fleas): *Bosmina*, *Chydorus*, *Daphnia* and *Simocephalus*

1 mm   0.3 mm   2.5 mm

COPEPODS: *Canthocamptus*, *Cyclops* with egg-sacs   and *Diaptomus*

1 mm long   1.5 mm long

Water slater, *Asellus aquaticus*
15 mm long

Approx. 17 mm long

Freshwater shrimp, *Gammarus pulex*

Freshwater crayfish, *Austro-potamobius pallipes*

Approx. 100 mm long

7 mm long

Fish louse, *Argulus foliaceus*

Fig. 10 Crustaceans. The water-fleas and copepods are tiny but numerous; they are an important part of the diet of growing fish. Argulus *species are external parasites on fish. Water slaters and freshwater shrimps are scavengers and predators on smaller invertebrates; they are eaten by fish. The British freshwater crayfish,* Austropotamobius pallipes *(previously called* Astacus*), a ravenous carnivore, is sought by pike and trout but has been reduced in numbers in the Bristol Avon above Chippenham by a fungus disease*

26

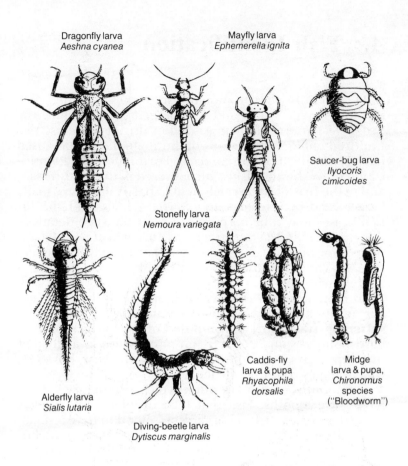

Dragonfly larva
Aeshna cyanea

Mayfly larva
Ephemerella ignita

Saucer-bug larva
Ilyocoris cimicoides

Stonefly larva
Nemoura variegata

Alderfly larva
Sialis lutaria

Diving-beetle larva
Dytiscus marginalis

Caddis-fly larva & pupa
Rhyacophila dorsalis

Midge larva & pupa,
Chironomus species
("Bloodworm")

Fig. 11 Aquatic larvae of insects. Insect larvae, particularly so-called 'bloodworms', may be mistaken for worms, but are more highly organized. The head is distinctive, having antennae, eyes and biting mouth-parts; below it is a thorax (chest), usually bearing three pairs of legs or some stubby false legs; and below this the abdomen takes the form of up to ten rounded segments, some of these (and particularly the lowest) often equipped with appendages for breathing and attachment. Some larvae develop by moulting their skins; others mature by pupating, i.e. enveloping themselves in a cocoon while their wings develop. Insect larvae play important roles in the freshwater drama of eating and being eaten

4. Fish Identification

The scientific classification of fishes takes account of fish throughout the world and is arranged so as to show the probable pattern of their evolution during the past five hundred million years. Many of the anatomical details used in that classification are internal. Fortunately the identification of freshwater fishes encountered in the British Isles, and in the Bristol Avon catchment in particular, can usually be achieved by reference to external details. Only in difficult cases may it be necessary to ascertain such details as the number and arrangement of throat teeth – as happened, for instance, in 1973 when a large pinkish dace-like fish was caught in the Winford Brook: it proved to be a golden orfe.

Prominent in external features are the number, shape and position of the fins and how they are stiffened. The stiffening framework is composed of rays, which may be hard-pointed spines, or soft and more or less branched at their tips. Rays sometimes branch from the base, however, which makes counting difficult.

The mouths of fish are often typical. Predatory species have large mouths. Fish that feed on plankton – that is small floating or drifting organisms – tend to have a small, upwardly directed mouth at the end of the snout, but bottom feeding kinds have the mouth situated beneath the head, and often of a protrusible construction like a suction pipe for searching the bottom. Bottom-feeders may also have barbels (sometimes called wattles) around the mouth, the number being characteristic of the species; barbels are organs of touch that reveal the presence of food.

The bodies of most fish are covered with scales (bullheads, 'leather' carp and lampreys are exceptions). The scales of our freshwater fish may be cycloid (thin and more or less rounded, as on carp and pike) or ctenoid (comb-like, as on perch). Scales remain constant in number and grow in size by the addition of plates as the fish grows; whether a fish has many small scales or fewer large ones is a characteristic of its species. They can be counted along the lateral line. (Scales along the lateral line can be distinguished because they each carry a tiny pore that leads to a sensory canal running beneath the skin.)

Proportions of the body are subtle, but comparative depth of body may be measured by counting diagonally the number of scales from the leading edge of the dorsal fin down to the lateral line, and again from the lateral line down to the attachment of the ventral fin. ('Ventral' fin is a traditional term meaning 'on the belly', but in some kinds of fish these fins are forward of the belly, so zoologists prefer the term 'pelvic' fin.)

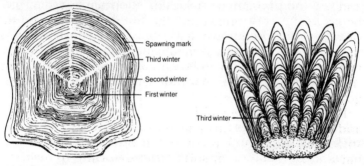

Fig. 12 Cycloid scale of roach and ctenoid (comb-like) scale of perch, showing annual growth. The surface of a scale is marked by ridges, more or less concentric around the point of origin. The ridges are formed in the course of outward growth and are widely spaced in summer, narrowly spaced in winter; under a low-power microscope they can be seen in distinct bands from which the age of the fish may be deduced. Occasions of spawning are shown by irregular erosion of a ridge. Perch scales are eroded also at their origins, so two years may be added to allow for this when counting the number of winter bands

In classifying living things, large or small, the basic unit is the species – a term that has already been used in this book but without explanation. A species may be defined as a recognizable sort of plant or animal that is able to reproduce among its own kind consistently true to type. Dace consistently breed dace, and dace is a species. Similar but slightly different species that are believed to have evolved from a common ancestor are grouped together into a genus. Dace, chub and orfe are members of the same genus (plural genera). Several genera may be grouped into a family, in this case the carp family; and so on to larger groupings – order, class, phylum, kingdom.

29

The use of English fish names is not always consistent. What we call rudd in England are called roach in Ireland. The Continental wels or waller is also called sheet-fish and catfish, but we must be careful to say European catfish, because there are American catfish that are very different, and marine catfish that are not even remotely related. Further confusion surrounds marine catfish, for they are sold in fried-fish shops under the name of rock salmon, though they have no relation to the salmon family! By international convention, scientists all over the world have resolved the problem of names by adopting a system promoted in the 18th century by the Swedish naturalist Carl Linné – otherwise known as Carolus Linnaeus because in his time Latin was the universal language of men of learning. Linnaeus himself named and described in Latin some 7,700 species of plants and 4,400 species of animals.

The name of each species is made up of two parts: the generic name (beginning with a capital letter) and what is called the trivial name (with no capital), rather like a person's name consisting of a surname and a forename. Linnaeus named dace as *Leuciscus leuciscus*, chub as *Leuciscus cephalus*, orfe as *Leuciscus idus*. Repetition of the generic name in the trivial name shows without further words that this species is typical of the genus.

Names of zoological families end in -idae; the generic name of carp is *Cyprinus*, the common carp is *Cyprinus carpio* and the carp family is known as the Cyprinidae.

As knowledge increases, a species is sometimes reclassified into a new or related genus. Linnaeus placed all the mayflies he knew in the genus *Ephemera*, but his two-winged mayfly *Ephemera diptera* is now known as *Chloëon dipterum* (Linn.), meaning 'two-winged olive mayfly', the addition in brackets indicating an alteration. Specialists cannot always agree whether slight but consistent variants from type deserve the status of separate species. Some lump all the variants into one species, as Tate Regan did with *Salmo trutta*; others split them into distinct species, unfortunately in a few instances creating alternative names in spite of the international rules.

A scheme for finding the name of any species of freshwater fish found in the Bristol Avon or its tributaries is set out in Appendix 1.

30

5. Primitive Fishes

The roundmouths (previously called Cyclostomata but renamed Marsipobranchii on account of their pouch gills) are a class of animals so primitive as scarcely to be called fish. They comprise lampreys (freshwater and marine species) and hag-fishes (which are marine). Lampreys look eel-like, but they are much less developed than eels, for the skeleton is cartilaginous and they are quite devoid of limbs, ribs, jaws and scales. The mouth is round, a veritable suction disc armed with rasping teeth. Pouch-like gills provide for respiration, water being passed in and out through six or seven external gill-slits on each side of the neck.

The sea lamprey (*Petromyzon marinus*), about two feet in length, and the lampern or river lamprey (*Lampetra fluviatilis*), half that size, regularly move up the Severn estuary to spawn in fresh water, and it is possible that some may find their way into the Avon estuary; they might even have penetrated to the freshwater river in the days when there were no weirs to bar their progress. More certainty attaches to the brook lamprey (*Lampetra planeri*), which is found in river gravels of the Avon and its major tributaries. Brook lampreys are wholly freshwater in their habits. They are of the thickness and length of a new pencil, olive-coloured on the back but pale on the belly, and have two shallow dorsal fins that look like a ridge running down the

Fig. 13 The brook lamprey, Lampetra planeri. *This is the smallest of the three British lampreys. Unlike the other two, it spends all its life in fresh water, and is found in river gravels where the hill streams begin to flatten out into lowland river*

31

lower part of the back to the pointed tail. The round mouth armed with teeth is slightly down-pointing, the eyes are rather protruding and there are seven roundish gill-openings on each side behind the head.

Brook lampreys congregate in springtime and communally clear a patch of gravel for spawning by lifting stones and other obstructions into the current, using their suctorial mouths. Then, by undulating their bodies, they plough furrows in which the females deposit small masses of tiny eggs. These are immediately fertilized by male milt and promptly covered with silt by more body undulations. The eggs hatch in about a fortnight, producing worm-like larvae known as prides or ammocoetes – the latter a name originally given them when they were thought to be a distinct species of animal. At this stage the mouth is a mere slit fringed with small barbels, the eyes are minute, and in place of gill-openings there is a narrow groove. The ammocoetes live in mud and ingest any organic matter it contains, until after three years they become adults, free-swimming and predatory on bottom fauna, including fish spawn and small fish, to which they attach themselves by their suctorial mouths.

Members of the next class up in the evolution of fish show much more elaboration of structure and function and are known as the Chondrichthyes or cartilaginous fishes. There is a well-developed skeleton made of cartilage (gristle), there are paired pectoral and pelvic (ventral) fins, upper and lower jaws, elongated gill-openings, and the body is covered with a tough skin in which plate-like scales are embedded. The class includes (a) sharks and dogfishes, (b) rays and skates and (c) rabbit-fishes. There are no British freshwater examples, but it is reported that freshwater sharks are to be found in lakes in Nicaragua and the Philippines. However, the lesser-spotted dogfish (*Scyliorhinus caniculus*) and various species of ray frequent the Bristol Channel and may occasionally be swept by the tide into the Avon estuary. The rays are known locally as 'skate', but strictly speaking only the common skate (*Raja batis*) is entitled to that name; it may be distinguished by its diamond shape, long narrow tail, smooth skin, grey coloration with ringed marks on its upper surface and its characteristic bluish under-surface. Other rays may be rounder in outline, have rough or spiny skins, and white or grey under-surfaces.

Modern Fishes

The third and most numerous class is that of the true bony fishes, previously named Osteoichthyes, but now simply called Pisces. They have not only a skeleton of real bone and paired limb-like fins but they have gills protected by a gill-cover opening to the exterior on each side of the head, the skin is normally covered with scales and they usually possess a swim-bladder for controlled buoyancy. The Bristol Avon catchment holds 15 native species of freshwater bony fish and (including two found in ornamental ponds) some 9 introduced species. They fall into eight families, as described in the following chapters.

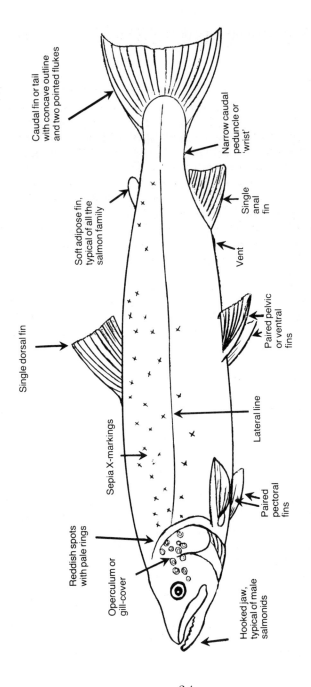

Caudal fin or tail with concave outline and two pointed flukes

Narrow caudal peduncle or 'wrist'

Single anal fin

Vent

Soft adipose fin, typical of all the salmon family

Single dorsal fin

Paired pelvic or ventral fins

Lateral line

Sepia X-markings

Paired pectoral fins

Reddish spots with pale rings

Operculum or gill-cover

Hooked jaw, typical of male salmonids

Fig. 14 External features of a fish: in this example a male salmon, Salmo salar

34

6.   The Salmon Family

Members of the salmon family rank among the most graceful, vigorous and interesting of fishes. They are all distinguished by having a small soft appendage, unstiffened by spines or rays and called the adipose fin, situated on the back between the dorsal fin and the tail. In the British Isles the family includes the Atlantic salmon (*Salmo salar*) and a number of fish grouped under the names of brown and sea trout (*Salmo trutta*), rainbow trout (*Salmo gairdneri*), grayling (*Thymallus thymallus*), char (*Salvelinus* species) and whitefish (*Coregonus* species). Rainbow trout are not native but are of North American origin, and in the Bristol Avon catchment are perpetuated by artificial rearing. The chars and the variously named whitefish (vendace, pollan, powan, schelly, gwyniad, houting) are upland lake fish not found in the Bristol Avon catchment. The fish we buy as tinned salmon also belong to this family but to a Pacific genus, *Oncorhynchus*, of which there are five species of commercial importance.

Salmon and Sea Trout

It is doubtful whether the Bristol Avon was ever a proper salmon river or indeed if Bristol apprentices really were surfeited with cheap salmon dinners. In the years 1656-85 when John Aubrey was writing his *Memoires of Naturall Remarques in the County of Wilts*, he recorded occasional salmon in 'the Upper Avon' (by which he meant the Salisbury Avon). In 'the North Avon' (meaning our river) he recorded 'troutes', 'carpes which are extraordinary good' and 'very good perches'; and 'good pikes, roches and daces in both the Avons'. But he made no mention of salmon in our river, a thing he would have known and made a note of had there been any in his time.

In *The New History, Survey & Description of the City & Suburbs of Bristol*, published in 1794, William Matthews wrote that 'the Avon is clear and shallow at low water, deep and muddy at high water ... This River ... yeilds some salmon, shads, plaise, flounders, sand'dabs, plenty of eels

35

and immense quantities of elvers'; but were his salmon always salmon or were they sometimes sea trout?

Presenting a report in June 1868, Mr. Walpole, one of Her Majesty's Inspectors of Fisheries under the Salmon Fishery Act of 1861, stated that 'the Bristol Channel is fully stocked with salmon as well as the tide-ways of the Parret and Avon', and 'notwithstanding the impediments which exist, salmon have been known to ascend the Avon to above Bristol, to the weir at Keynsham, thirteen miles from the [Severn] estuary, above which they are excluded by unsurmountable weirs'. If these salmon he writes of could not reach their spawning grounds farther up-river, could they properly have been Avon salmon or were they more probably strays from the Severn, Wye or Usk?

In *A Handy Guide to the Fishing near Bath*, 'Piscator' (a pen name for William Hiskey) wrote in 1881 that 'salmon are said to have been taken within living memory but now are certainly merely a tradition'. *A Handy Guide to Fishing in the Neighbourhood of Bristol*, published in 1887 and possibly by the same author, says:

> Years ago the winding Avon was doubtless a salmon river. Even now an occasional sickly salmon is found as far up the river as Netham, and scarcely a season passes without half-a-dozen being picked up in the river when very high tides and plenty of rain have tempted them up to sicken and die as soon as they meet the poisonous refuse discharged into the tide from sewers and factories.

Similarities and differences between salmon, sea trout and other trout have not always been clearly defined nor properly appreciated. Capt. Frank Buckland, one of the early Inspectors of Salmon Fisheries, used to tell a story of some netsmen who had captured a nondescript salmonid. One said it was a kelt (a spent salmon), another that it was a finnock (sea trout), a third that it was a bull trout (estuary trout); to which the leader replied, 'Nay, in the London fish market it will be a salmon'. I myself have seen sea trout labelled salmon on a fishmonger's slab.

In 1880, the Keeper of Zoology at the British Museum, Dr. A. C. G. Günther, describing fishes of the British Isles, listed Atlantic salmon and ten allegedly distinct species of trout. It was not until the early years of the 20th century that Dr. Charles Tate Regan, again at the British Museum, sorted out the salmonids and concluded that in spite of great differences in coloration the ten trouts – particularly brown and sea trout – are all the same species, a conclusion that is accepted by most authorities today.

Further doubt if the Bristol Avon used to be a salmon river before weirs and pollution modified it is cast by the absence of large holding pools such as are typical of salmon rivers elsewhere, and a lack of coarse gravels such as salmon are known to favour for spawning on – deep beds of pebbles at least as big as marbles, kept free of silt deposits and constantly oxygenated by a strong flow of clean water. In a discussion on the absence of salmon from certain clean rivers, Dr. J. W. Jones of Liverpool University, a trustworthy expert on the Atlantic salmon, has said that spawning salmon, which are largish fish, say 10-20 pounds in weight, need at least 6-9 inches depth of water to work in, so as to bury their eggs some 9-12 inches deep in gravel. To assist the digging of a redd (spawning bed) and to keep silt from subsequently smothering the eggs, he said, water speed must be of the order of 1 to 1.5 feet per second. Here in the Bristol Avon catchment our headsprings are numerous but small, spread over the wide rims of saucer-like beds of alternating clay and limestone; the springs seldom yield both the required depth and the required speed. Ours are not mountain rivers but hill streams, slower, shallower and with finer gravels, which we know are suitable for being cut into by spawning brown trout. In spite of the wet-weather spates that farther downstream bring deposits of clay to fill empty spaces and smother fish eggs, at least near the headsprings trout eggs are fairly sure of successful incubation.

Hearsay reports of salmonids occasionally found stranded around the mouth of the Avon are guarded. These fish might properly belong to the Usk, Wye or Severn catchments and could be either salmon or sea trout. More certainty attaches to the large silvery fish we know about that during the second half of the 20th century have managed to penetrate through the Avon estuary under favourable conditions of spring tide and wet-weather flow,

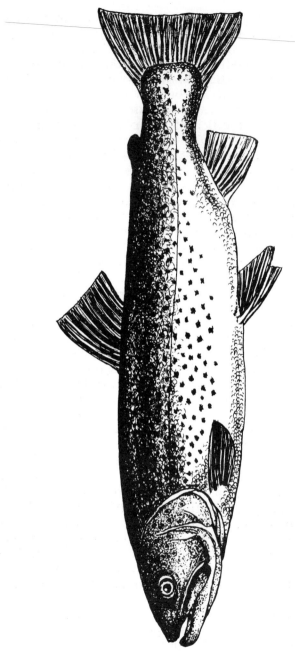

Fig. 15 Sea trout, Salmo trutta. In comparison with salmon, sea trout have a greater depth of body relative to length; this is especially noticeable in the caudal peduncle or 'wrist'

and have been observed and caught with rod and line at Keynsham and Bath and even farther upstream. These fish have been carefully inspected and recorded by the Bristol Avon Area Fish Records Panel, working in very close collaboration with the Bristol Avon River Board and its successors.

How are sea trout and salmon distinguished, one from the other? Although salmon grow to larger sizes than sea trout, they are much more elegantly modelled, sea trout being comparatively thick-set. The peduncle or 'wrist' of a salmon's tail, for instance, is slender – only one-third as deep as the tail flukes from point to point – whereas a sea trout's peduncle is nearly one-half that depth. A salmon's flukes are subtly concave, and each terminates neatly in an acute angle, whereas a sea trout's tail ends in a nearly straight line, with no suggestion of a cleft, and its angles are squarer. The differences give the salmon not only greater muscle-power but a better grip on the water and therefore greater speed to cover greater distances and make higher leaps. Nevertheless, a sea trout is no sluggard.

Other noticeable differences are that in salmon the dorsal fin has more soft branched rays (10-12, rarely 9) than in trout (8-10, rarely 11). In adult salmon the anal fin is less pointed than in trout, and if laid back against the body the last fin ray (i.e. nearest the tail) will protrude farther than the longest ray in that fin, whereas in trout the longest ray of the anal fin laid back extends farther than the most posterior ray. Scales on the wrist of the tail are larger but fewer in salmon (10-13 obliquely from the base of the adipose fin down to the lateral line) than in trout (13-16).

Coloration is not conclusive, but sea trout are usually silvery all over, with large sepia-coloured, squarish or X-shaped markings, in contrast with tiny dark speckles on the steel-blue sides of salmon, or the wide range of circular red and black spots faintly ringed with white superimposed on the golden to black shading of a brown trout. As is usual with fish, the backs of salmon, sea trout and brown trout are all darker than the sides, and the bellies are paler, almost white.

The records of the one-time Avon, Brue & Parret Fishery Board (sic, though the usual spelling is now Parrett) included a report of a 3 lb sea trout caught in the Bristol

Avon at Swineford in 1887 and another report of a 9¼ lb trout caught at Bathampton in 1897 which, from its size, might well have been a sea trout. Interest revived in June 1952 when a run of undoubted sea trout penetrated the Bristol Avon as far as the Colour Mill pool on the River Chew in what is now Keynsham Park; there were estimated to be twenty of them, at least 2 lb (nearly 1 kg) each, and on 28th June, Mr. Brian Veale of Keynsham caught one by rod and line, weighing 6 lb (2.722 kg). On 12th September 1958, Mr. Tom Cleary caught a sea trout weighing 5 lb 1½ oz (2.311 kg) on the Bristol Avon just upstream of Bathampton Weir, and on 26th September the same year, Mr. F. J. Greenland caught a sea trout of 6 lb 12 oz (3.062 kg) even farther upstream, in the Cam Brook just above Midford. During the early spring of 1960 a run of school peal, i.e. young sea trout, was observed in the Avon at Saltford; five of them were caught, aggregating 9 lb (4 kg). In 1961, there was no observed run, but 'bush telegraph' gave news of an alleged 4 lb sea trout caught at Hanham. The largest sea trout yet on record for the Bristol Avon was caught with rod and line at Twerton, Bath, on 30th June 1964, by a schoolboy, Martin Bowler; it weighed 6 lb 12¾ oz (3.083 kg) and its scales indicated an age of 6 years plus, with three years spent in fresh water and three in the estuary. On 12th September 1965, a school of peal was sighted in the tidal Avon at Hotwells, Bristol, and later the same year a few sea trout of 4-5 lb (2 kg) were observed in the freshwater river between Hanham and Saltford. In the following years, notably 1966-68, a few school peal were again observed in the Hanham-Saltford stretch. (1968 must have been a good year for up-river migrants; May 1968 had a remarkable run of elvers at Keynsham Weir.) On 12th August 1970, a 12 lb (5.5 kg) salmon was found dead on the estuarial mud near Gaol Ferry Bridge, Bristol. On 4th May 1979, Mr. Roger Smith of Bath caught a sea trout weighing 6 lb 10 oz (3.005 kg) in the Avon at Pulteney Weir.

Because weirs present major obstructions to fish migrating up-river, the Bristol Avon River Authority made it a matter of policy (which has been accepted by its successor, the Wessex Water Authority) to incorporate a fish pass in any major weir needing reconstruction; this was done in the Bath flood-protection scheme, passes being installed at Pulteney Weir and Twerton, completed in 1973. A temporary fish pass of timber was also built on to the existing Keynsham Weir in 1972; this is presently (1987) being replaced by a permanent structure.

The life history of Atlantic salmon is generally well known; that of sea trout is similar, the main differences being (*a*) when they drop down-river and go to sea, salmon go farther out and to deeper water, where they can enjoy a rich diet of small sea fish, but sea trout hang around the estuaries, where the diet is better than in fresh water but more limited than that in the open sea; (*b*) mature salmon are larger than mature sea trout; (*c*) unlike salmon, sea trout continue to feed after they have re-entered fresh water; and (*d*) salmon spawn on beds of pebbles scoured by deep and strongly flowing water, whereas sea trout spawn on finer gravels scoured by shallower and less strong flows.

Sea trout have usually spent two years in the freshwater river and one year in the saline estuary (in this case the Bristol Channel) when they begin to feel the urge to reproduce. It is believed that they recognize and proceed up the river of their origin by following subtle scents called pheromones that are secreted by their fellows upstream, but with the extraordinary tidal movements of the Bristol Channel and the several rivers that empty into it there must be a large element of chance in where they are heading. Aided by favourable tides and seasonal rainfall, they move up-river in early spring or late summer to find beds of fine gravel near the headsprings about November, but it can be earlier or later, as the weather (and particularly temperature) is a controlling factor. Having selected a place for her redd, a female sea trout turns on her side and undulates her body to make the current carry gravel particles away. She hovers over the hollow thus created, while a male positions himself just upstream. Suddenly she sheds her ripe eggs (ova) into the redd, the male sheds milt (sperms) among them, and the female immediately undulates upstream to divert further particles to cover the eggs in the hollow, where the wriggling sperms rapidly seek and penetrate them to effect fertilization, the eggs swelling meanwhile until they look very much like halibut-oil cap-

41

sules. The spawning process is repeated several times, the redds showing up as small patches of disturbance on the slightly silted stream bottom. A female sea trout yields nearly a thousand eggs per pound of body-weight, but by contrast with other freshwater fish families this is not a large number. Having achieved their purpose, spent fish drop down-river, and the more fortunate sea trout might reach the estuary to recuperate, but weakened by swimming and spawning most of them are potential victims for gulls and other predators.

Sea-trout eggs are heavier than water, so stay put in the gravel, but there is inevitably predation by water birds, eels and other fish, and the larger insect larvae. Incubation is sensitive to temperature, usually taking from three weeks to three months, according to the severity of the winter. If deprived of dissolved oxygen, as can happen by smothering with mud, eggs die and their albumen coagulates to an opaque white. In a live fertilized egg an eye-spot presently shows that development is proceeding; then an S-shaped embryo becomes apparent and eventually there emerges from the egg a larval fish about half an inch long (12 mm) called an alevin. Attached to its belly is a yolk-sac filled with oily matter that for the next ten days or so will be used as food while the alevin learns to struggle out of the gravel and forage for diatoms, protozoans and other microscopic particles. By the time the alevin has doubled its length and begun to feed on bottom-living invertebrates it looks like a real fish, generally olive-coloured but with a sheen, and marked with speckles and on each side about a dozen large, vertically oval smudges alternating with reddish spots faintly ringed with white. The smudges are called parr marks, and as long as it has them the young fish is called a parr. A parr usually remains in fresh water for two years (in colder latitudes possibly longer), feeding on progressively larger organisms such as freshwater shrimps and snails, and reaching a length of about 8 inches (20 cm). Eventually the general colour turns silvery, the parr marks fade (but not the speckles), the pectoral fins become orange-coloured, and the anal fin assumes a white leading edge backed by a darker band. The young fish is then known as a smolt and is ready for seaward migration. This takes place about April or May, the smolt being carried down-river over weirs tail-first. Sometimes young sea trout return up-river as orange-fins after less than a year in salt water.

As with salmon, the main events of a sea trout's life are recorded on the scales, those at the shoulder being the most legible. Reminiscent of the annual growth rings of tree trunks, times of slow growth in the winter and faster growth in summer result in thinner and thicker additions to a scale, seen in plan as closely spaced contour lines and wider bands respectively; periods of good feeding in the sea show up as even wider bands. Spawning causes irregular erosion of the plates of which the scale is built up.

To sum up at this point: (a) it would seem that at some time in the past the Bristol Avon was a sea-trout river, not a salmon river, though salmon properly belonging to other Bristol Channel rivers sometimes might have and may still come up the Bristol Avon estuary. (b) In the 19th and 20th centuries obstructive weirs and gross water pollution made fish migration through the estuary well-nigh impossible, and the Bristol Avon strain of sea trout has died out. (c) In the second half of the 20th century the Avon estuary has been progressively cleared of its municipal and industrial pollution, and weirs are being made passable by the installation of fish passes. (d) As a result of Tate Regan's studies it is generally accepted that sea trout are a strain of brown trout, *Salmo trutta*, that have inherited a sea-going habit.

The question now arises: will the Bristol Avon again become a sea-trout river? If the physical conditions are again suitable, how can the river be recolonized with its own strain of sea trout? The hope that Bristol Avon brown trout might forage sufficiently far down-river to discover the advantages of estuarial feeding and then return in sufficient numbers to reproduce a sea-going strain is doomed to failure because fishing pressure is too severe and likely to remain so. Another possibility is that sea trout from other Bristol Channel rivers might wander into the Avon in sufficient numbers to spawn there and establish a Bristol Avon strain of sea trout. Given time, this could happen, though the chance is slim because sea trout ascending the Avon are every angler's game. The idea could be tried out, with the aid of a byelaw ban on taking sea trout, for an experimental period, say up to the year 2000. A

43

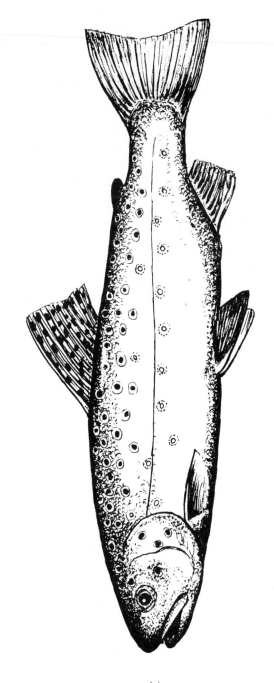

Fig. 16 Brown trout, Salmo trutta

44

third possibility is to incubate known sea-trout eggs from another catchment area and rear the resulting parr artificially until they are big enough, at about 18 months, to plant into the Bristol Avon hill streams. Such a possibility is within the capabilities of the regional Water Authority.

Brown Trout

The next fish for consideration here is a less speculative subject, though one of management concern to the regional Water Authority and fishing associations because of its exacting water requirements and the fishing pressure put upon it. The Bristol Avon holds brown trout, *Salmo trutta*, practically throughout its freshwater length; so do most of the tributaries and some of the lakes, notably Chew Valley Lake, where the large numbers of splendid fish taken by anglers are replenished by artificial rearing and restocking. Trout seem to be very much at home in the hill streams, but as they grow larger they tend to drop downstream to more spacious waters in the Avon, though returning to the hill streams to spawn.

Structurally, brown trout are the same as sea trout, already described, but generally they are smaller because they do not have the benefit of good feeding in sea water. To date the largest brown trout taken by rod and line in the Bristol Avon was one of 7 lb 1 oz (3.204 kg) captured in 1977 at Saltford by Mr. R. Chedzoy; the largest brown trout from Chew Valley Lake, where the feeding is remarkably good, was taken in 1968 by Mr. R. R. Browning and weighed 10 lb 12 oz (4.876 kg). In the hill streams a large proportion of brown trout are of small size because they have not finished growing. The legal minimum takeable size for the Bristol Avon catchment is 25 centimetres (10 inches) measured from the tip of the snout to the fork or cleft of the tail, and there is a catch limit of two trout per person per day. (By written dispensation from the Water Authority, this may be increased for private waters that are restocked.)

The coloration of fish is seldom a precise characteristic. In brown trout it may range from sepia to light olive-brown on the back, from silver to gold on the flanks and from apricot to white on the belly, but this basic colour may be

45

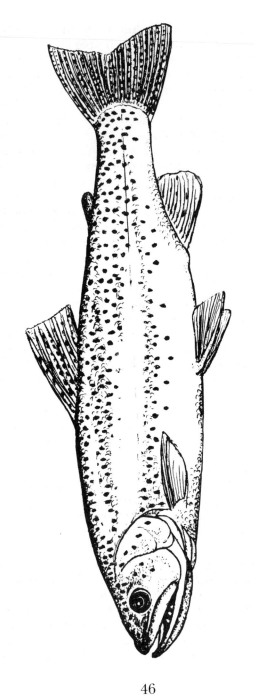

Fig. 17 Rainbow trout, Salmo gairdneri

tinted with almost any other colour in an artist's palette, and superimposed on the back and sides are many spots, sepia or red, large and small, round or jagged, sometimes ringed with white or grey. The silvery whiteness seen on the belly and sides of fish is due to guanin, a crystallized waste product in temporary storage. There are also three pigments in the epidermal cells: melanin (black), carotene (red) and xanthophyll (yellow). To these all the colours of the rainbow may be subtly added by diffraction of light at and just below the surface of the body. The blobs of pigment in each cell are expanded or contracted in response to nervous impulses, for purposes of concealment or display; in trout the overall effect is camouflage, whether on a pebbly or muddy bottom, in gloomy depths or flashing, broken water. On young brown trout the smudgy parr marks may be faint or dark, but the white-ringed red spots between the parr marks show up conspicuously when the fish is taken out of the water.

The life history of brown trout is similar to that of sea trout except that brown trout do not habitually migrate to and from the estuary. Brown trout usually spawn in November and December, so the statutory close season for taking non-migratory trout with rod and line in the Bristol Avon catchment has been fixed as the period between 15th October and 1st April following – or in the case of reservoirs, lakes and ponds (where close supervision of stocks is usually exercised) 17th March. The food of brown trout progresses from diatoms and small crustaceans at the alevin stage to insect larvae, fish eggs (including trout eggs), adult insects, freshwater shrimps, tadpoles, water snails, sticklebacks and the fry of other fishes, frogs and even small mammals such as water shrews.

Rainbow Trout

The rainbow trout, *Salmo gairdneri*, is a fish of western North America, a species as diverse in habits and appearance as our own *Salmo trutta*. What we know today as rainbow trout appear to be the results of interbreeding between at least two strains or subspecies: the non-migratory Sacramento rainbow, *Salmo gairdneri shasta* (which normally spawns November-December), and the migratory

47

steelhead trout, *Salmo gairdneri irideus* (which returns from the Pacific coast to spawn up-river February-May). These hybrids were introduced to Japan in 1877, Germany in 1882 and Great Britain in 1884, and have become popular for supplying fishmongers and hoteliers with table fish. They grow faster than our native brown trout, but when planted into local rivers seldom stay where put, scattering at random near and far within the catchment basin in very few days and ultimately going seaward if not captured. In confined waters rainbow trout do very well. Chew Valley Lake, for instance, is annually stocked with rainbow trout from the Bristol Waterworks Company's own fish hatchery at Ubley, nearby, where selected mature fish are spawned artificially. The largest rainbow trout caught there to date was one of 13 lb 3 oz (5.982 kg) taken by Mr. B. Bennett in 1984. For the Bristol Avon the record to date is one of 5 lb 15 oz 8 drm (2.707 kg) taken on fly by Mr. R. Ford at Somerford in 1974.

A mature rainbow trout is at once distinguishable from a brown or sea trout by a broad band of purple (brighter in the males) stretching along each side of the silvery body, and by many small blackish spots scattered from head to tail and even on the fins. The overall coloration is variable, however; one sees steel-blue specimens that must be throw-backs to steelhead parentage. A red slash sometimes seen beneath the jaw is not a deformity but an indication of a third subspecies of rainbow in the individual's ancestry, the cut-throat trout. Other distinguishing features of rainbow trout are 4 hard and 9-10 soft rays in the dorsal fin, and 3 hard and 9-11 soft rays in the anal fin. The tail fin is shallowly indented, the angles of its flukes being about 60°. The lateral line comprises 120-150 small scales.

At Chew Valley Lake the rainbow trout are usually ready for spawning early in the new year. Variations in spawning times are attributable to mixed origins rather than to weather. In the Bristol Avon catchment, rainbow trout are now subject to the same close season as non-migratory trout (the period between 15th October and 1st April following) except in reservoirs, lakes and ponds, where the second date is 17th March and if there are no other species of fish therein the statutory close season is not applicable. The minimum takeable size for rainbow trout in the Bristol

Avon catchment is the same as for other trout, namely 25 centimetres (10 inches).

Brook Trout

Attempts were made in the late 1950s and early 1960s to establish the American 'brook trout' (properly a char, *Salvelinus fontinalis*) in Chew Valley Lake, but it became apparent that this could not be done in competition with native brown trout.

Grayling

The grayling (*Thymallus thymallus*) is a fish of fast-flowing well-oxygenated rivers, and because this is an exact requirement its distribution in mainland Britain is irregular. (Its absence from Ireland is another story that is set in Britain's ice ages.) The grayling is found in some of the gravelly stretches of the Bristol Avon above Melksham and in the larger tributaries, notably the River Chew. Its distribution may once have been more widespread (the Somerset Frome is said to have been a good grayling river within living memory), but pollution incidents about the time of the 1939-45 war are believed to have been responsible for its decline. Angling organizations have since attempted to make good such loss by restocking from the Salisbury Avon and Test catchments.

Grayling are truly beautiful fish, generally silver-grey in colour but tinted with iridescent green and purple, lightly sprinkled with small sepia spots on their very regular hex-

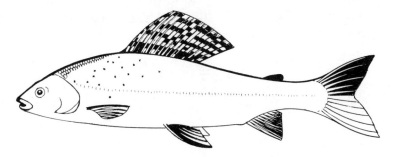

Fig. 18 Grayling, Thymallus thymallus

agonal scales. Besides having on its back the little adipose fin that shows it to be a member of the salmon family, a grayling carries a huge rhomboidal dorsal fin, stiffened by 4-7 hard and 13-17 branched rays and usually chequered in black, green and purple. When fully erected, this fin may seem disproportionately large, but like the keel of a boat this is a mechanism for directing available force to secure optimum speed. The tail fin is forked.

Unlike other native salmonids, the grayling spawns in springtime (March-May), the female shedding about 2,000 eggs per pound of body-weight into a redd hollowed in the gravel, rather as trout do. By contrast with eggs of most other freshwater fish, those of grayling are large (about a quarter-inch or 6 millimetres in diameter) and fewer in number. Not all are fertilized and many are destroyed by predators. Incubation takes two or three weeks, depending on water temperature, and the emerging alevins quickly use up their yolk-sacs and start feeding on microscopic plankton such as diatoms and newly hatched insects and crustaceans, which are plentiful at that time of year. (This may be the reason why grayling have evolved into spring spawners, from a family whose other members are autumn and winter spawners.) Adult grayling feed on insect larvae, freshwater shrimps and snails, but insects at the water surface also figure largely in their diet, and the larger grayling eat fish fry.

The statutory close season for taking grayling by rod and line in the Bristol Avon catchment is the same as for other freshwater fish, namely the period between 14th March and 16th June in each year. The largest grayling on record for the Bristol Avon is, to date, one weighing 2 lb 1 oz (0.936 kg) taken in 1986 by Mr. Laurence Pebworth at Somerford.

7. Shads

Shads are marine fish that belong to the herring family (Clupeidae), which has some affinity with salmonids. There are two British species, allis shad (*Alosa alosa*) and twaite shad (*Alosa fallax*), both of which look like overgrown herrings. In springtime they move into brackish or fresh water for spawning. They are not plentiful but are known to penetrate into the Severn estuary and to get as far up the freshwater river as Tewkesbury. Writing in 1794, before Netham Dam was made and the Avon estuary became polluted with municipal and industrial effluents, William Matthews recorded shads in the Avon estuary at Bristol. Now that the pollution is practically abated it is just possible that history will be repeated and that some shad may be found heading up the Bristol Avon. The species are described here for that reason.

Both shads have a single dorsal fin with only soft rays; the tail fin is deeply forked. There is no adipose fin, nor is there a lateral line. The mouth is terminal and reaches to the posterior side of the eye; the teeth are small and feeble. There are some radiating lines marked on the gillcovers.

Allis shad is the larger but rarer of the two species, growing up to 30 inches long and 8 lb in weight (76 cm, 3.6 kg). Twaite shad is smaller, no more than 20 inches long and 4 lb in weight (50 cm, 1.8 kg). The twaite shad carries a diminishing row of dark 'thumb marks' behind the head; the allis shad has these in youth but when adult retains only one such mark, just behind the gill-cover. An important distinction is found in the gill-rakers that lie under the gill-cover: on the first gill-arch, allis shad has 60-120 fine gill-rakers that are as long as or longer than the gills themselves, whereas twaite shad has only 20-45 gill-rakers that are stiff and shorter than the gills.

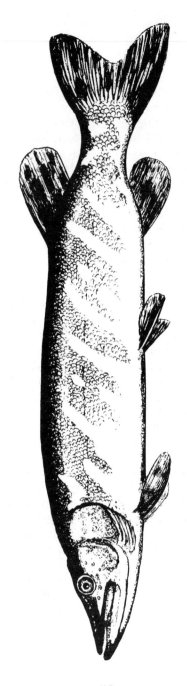

Fig. 19 Pike, Esox lucius

8. Pike

The pike family, Esocidae, has only one genus, and of its six species only one, the common pike (*Esox lucius*), is native to the British Isles and continental Europe, where it is widely distributed. It is encountered almost throughout the freshwater Bristol Avon, in the lower stretches of the tributaries, in the Kennet & Avon Canal and in many of the lakes, its usual haunts being weedy shallows and deep holes under a bank.

The very appearance of a pike denotes its predatory character: its head is strong-looking, long and vertically compressed; the mouth is wide, deeply cleft and armed with strong jaws and long hooked teeth (teeth even sprouting from the tongue); the all-seeing eyes lie high on the head, protected by sockets; the muscular body is long and narrow, but the belly is remarkably extensible. The fins are small and rounded, the single dorsal fin and the anal fin set well back towards the forked but well-rounded tail fin. The scales are small and neat, some 125-140 along the lateral line. The greenish body is splashed with white below and darkly shaded along the back, but the sides are flecked with creamy yellow, giving the effect of sunshine on vegetation.

Pike spawn early in the year, from February to May, in shallow water, a female being attended by two or three smaller males and shedding some 15,000 tiny eggs per pound of body-weight. The eggs lie around in clots for a while, but with rising temperatures they hatch within two or three weeks. Like other young fish, the offspring at first feed on small floating and bottom-living organisms, vegetable and animal, but on reaching a length of about 2 inches (5 cm) pike fry become wholly carnivorous, feeding on tadpoles and small fish and then progressing to bigger fish, water birds and small mammals. Wholly carnivorous fish such as pike and eels occupy high levels in the pattern of freshwater production, being exceeded only by warm-blooded animals, namely birds and mammals. Pike are credited with a feeding cycle of eleven days; if stories are to be believed, some of their larger victims could well take such a time to digest.

A young pike is properly called a pickerel, but anglers refer to a small pike under about 5 lb (2¼ kg) as a jack. The reading of scales taken from the shoulder to ascertain the age of pike is subject to a margin of error; alternative methods use the transmission of light through thin bony structures such as gill-covers or otoliths (ear-stones) ground to translucent thinness. It is not unusual for a pike to reach the age of 20 years, but contrary to popular legend pike seldom exceed 25 years. There are well-authenticated cases where pike have reached extraordinary sizes of the order of half a hundredweight (25 kg). The present British record for a rod-caught pike is 40 lb 0 oz (18.143 kg), established in 1967 by Mr. P. D. Hancock on Horsey Mere, Norfolk; in the Bristol Avon catchment the record rod-caught pike is one of 28 lb 0 oz (12.701 kg) taken in 1959 by Mr. A. E. Hall at Braydon Pond, near Malmesbury. The Bristol Avon itself has to date yielded a record pike of 22 lb 4 oz (10.092 kg) and the Kennet & Avon Canal one of 21 lb 0 oz (9.525 kg).

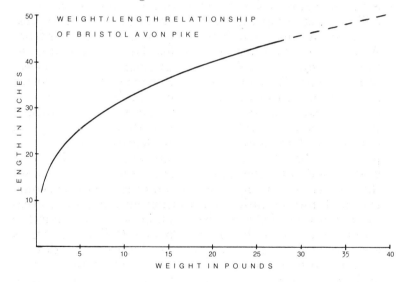

Fig. 20 The weight/length relationship of Bristol Avon pike conforms very closely to Mona's pike scale (Fishing Gazette, 1918), which is based on the assumption that weight is strictly proportional to the cube of the length. Attempts to plot a weight/age relationship, however, show a wide scatter, suggesting that some pike habitually feed better than others

9. The Common Eel

An eel is distinguished from other fish by having a mouth with jaws and teeth, an elongated, rather snake-like body with a long dorsal fin running down the back and usually confluent with a single-pointed tail, and an absence of any ventral (pelvic) fins. The European common eel, *Anguilla anguilla*, spends the greater part of its life in fresh water but is born at sea and returns there to spawn and die. The conger (*Conger conger*), wholly a sea fish, is a sort of cousin that zoologists now place in a separate family, and the moray (*Muraena helena*), wholly marine and seldom found as far north as the British Isles, is another relative now placed in yet another family. Sand-eels, both greater and lesser, are not related to the Anguillidae.

The remarkable story of freshwater eels migrating from the rivers of Europe to spawn in the deeps of the western Sargasso Sea is probably well known but always worthy of telling. Their offspring – or perhaps one should say successors, for they may include the progeny of contingents from American rivers – are tiny leaf-like larvae, once thought to be a distinct organism that was given the name *Leptocephalus*. They feed on microscopic marine plankton, grow, and coming nearer the surface are caught up in currents that carry some of them across the Atlantic towards Europe. By the time of arrival off the coasts they are three years old, of the shape and size of willow leaves, and still transparent so that their internal organs are visible. Then, in colder conditions, change occurs: they shrink to little more than 3 inches (7.5 cm) in length, and their bodies become rounded into the little semi-transparent but eel-like creatures that we call elvers. Elvers can be seen ascending the lower stretches of the Bristol Avon in billowing masses about the middle of May, whenever high spring tides are running to help them over Netham Dam, Hanham Weir and well up to if not actually over the crest of Keynsham Weir, where they continue to swarm, wriggling body over wriggling body, up the wet banks as the tide retreats. So they continue up-river and eventually disperse to slow or still waters in all parts of the catchment area, swimming

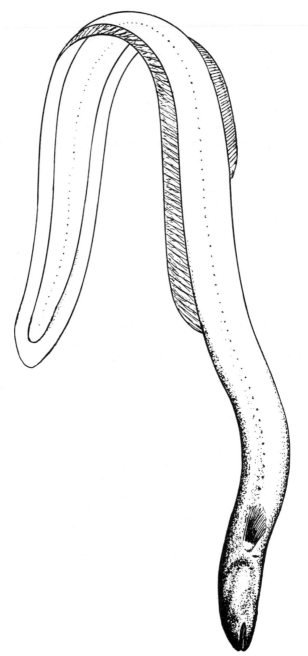

Fig. 21 Common eel, Anguilla anguilla

where they may and elsewhere wriggling overland through wet grass, even reaching ponds not connected to a river. Meanwhile the blood becomes red with haemoglobin to assist the supply of oxygen when they are out of water, and the body darkens, the flanks becoming olive-yellow, the back a darker olive-green.

Only the first half of an eel's body is truly circular in cross-section, the posterior half being laterally compressed. The mouth is small but bordered with large lips enclosing strong, widely opening jaws and tapering teeth. Ventral fins are conspicuously absent, but the anal fin is long, continuing from the middle of the body right to the tip of the tail, where it becomes continuous with the dorsal fin. The dorsal fin begins about a third of the body-length from the head, in this respect differing from that of a conger, which starts just above the tips of the pectorals, not far behind the head. An eel's skin is smooth and slimy, covered with little oval scales that do not overlap. Scales and ground-down otoliths (ear-stones) may be used to ascertain how many years have been spent in fresh water.

Adolescent eels feed voraciously, and usually by night, on any available animal diet: fish eggs and fry, insects and their larvae, freshwater shrimps, slaters and crayfish, snails and mussels, tadpoles, frogs and newts, larger fish, voles, and water birds of increasing sizes as growing appetites dictate. Male eels reach maturity after 5½-6½ years in fresh water, but females (which have broader heads and grow bigger) take longer, 6½-8½ years. As they approach maturity the colour of eels changes from their olive hues: the back becomes sepia-dark, the flanks bronzy and the belly silvery white. They are then called silver eels, and towards the end of summer they stop feeding and drop down-river to the sea and so to the Atlantic Ocean. When water mills were in active use nearly every mill weir had its 'cruive' or eel basket, a box of stout iron bars set into the weir crest to catch silver eels as they tailed down. With lack of attention these have fallen into disrepair, the last on the Bristol Avon being at Melksham Mill, dismantled in 1959 prior to weir reconstruction, and one at Saltford, recently refurbished.

Eels sometimes fail to go to sea on reaching what should be an age of maturity, but go on growing, the females in particular achieving remarkable stature. One such, caught in Bitterwell Lake, near Bristol, in 1922, established a British record; it weighed 8 lb 8 oz (3.856 kg) and was for many years on display at Veals' tackle shop in Bristol. This record was overtaken in 1969 by an eel caught by Mr. A. Dart in Hunstrete Lake, near Pensford, weighing 8 lb 10 oz (3.912 kg). The British record for a rod-caught eel has moved on to one of 11 lb 2 oz (5.046 kg) taken in 1978 by Mr. S. Terry at Kingfisher Lake, near Ringwood, Hants. The biggest eel to date taken by rod and line on the Bristol Avon weighed 3 lb 10 oz (1.644 kg), but this is exceeded by an eel of 3 lb 15 oz (1.786 kg) caught on the Somerset Frome.

10. The Carp Family

The carp family (Cyprinidae) is widely distributed throughout the world and consists mostly of freshwater fish. The fourteen species of cyprinids encountered in waters of the Bristol Avon catchment are as many as all the other fish species there put together, and collectively the fish of this family far outnumber and outweigh all the others.

A fish belonging to the carp family has only one dorsal fin; its paired pectoral fins are located rather low beneath the shoulder, and the paired ventral (pelvic) fins are placed about midway along the belly. There is no adipose fin. The body is fully covered with scales (leather carp and mirror carp being exceptions, explained later) and the lateral line can be observed running along each flank except possibly on minnows, where it sometimes peters out before reaching the tail. The mouth is extensible but has no teeth; one, two or three rows of teeth are, however, found in the throat on the lower pharyngeal bones, biting upwards against a hard palate. The number and arrangement of the teeth are a useful aid in identifying a specimen; in the following table the figures represent the numbers of teeth per row on both sides.

In one row	
Crucian carp and goldfish	4 and 4
Tench	4 and 5 or 5 and 4 (rarely 5 and 5)
Common bream	5 and 5
Roach	5 and 5 (sometimes 6 and 5)
In two rows	
Dace	2-5 and 5-2
Chub	2-5 and 5-2 (sometimes 5-1)
Minnow	2-4 and 4-2 (often 2-5 and 4-2)
Bleak	2-5 and 5-2
Gudgeon	2-5 and 5-2
Rudd	3-5 and 5-3
In three rows	
Common carp	1-1-3 and 3-1-1
Barbel	2-3-5 and 5-3-2

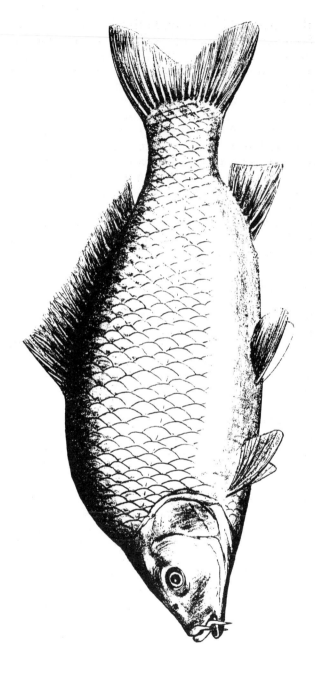

Fig. 22 Common or king carp, Cyprinus carpio

Most of the carp family feed on both vegetable and animal diets. Some bottom-feeding species have a number of wattles or barbels around the mouth to help detect and identify food: common carp and barbel have four, tench and gudgeon two.

In contrast to members of the salmon family, which are fast movers, have a high metabolic rate and need plenty of dissolved oxygen, members of the carp family have a reputation for lethargy; they are not exacting about dissolved oxygen levels and are comparatively slow-moving – unless endangered, when for short periods, with strong muscular sinuations and rapid tail-beats, they can attain speeds up to ten body-lengths per second.

A preliminary sorting of species is given in the identification chart of Appendix 1. Further descriptions are given under each species, as follows.

The Common Carp

The common or king carp (*Cyprinus carpio*) is not a true native of the British Isles but is believed to have originated in central Asia and to have been introduced to Europe and so to Britain from the vicinity of the Caspian Sea. It is really a pond fish, preferring warm and muddy-bottomed still water to flowing rivers, and it has been farmed for many centuries as well as naturalized in many parts of the world. In the Bristol Avon catchment it is very much at home in the Kennet & Avon Canal and most of the larger ponds, including the 'Capability' Brown lakes; it is also found in the slower stretches of the Avon and larger tributaries.

In appearance the common carp is muscular and rather thick-set, sometimes quite deep in the body if well fed, and it has a well-rounded back surmounted by a long dorsal fin consisting of three or four hard spines followed by about 20 soft branched rays. The anal fin is narrow, having only three hard and five soft rays, and the tail fin is well forked. The snout is conical, the small mouth down-turned but protrusible, and there are four barbels, i.e. two small and greyish sprouting from the upper lip and two longer and orange-coloured at the corners of the mouth. The general coloration varies somewhat from water to water,

61

but usually the back is of dark olive-brown, the flanks lighter and bronzy, the belly yellow, and there are tints of orange in the finnage. A resilient rim may be noticed around each gill-cover: this enables the carp to seal its gills against adverse conditions such as mud or drought, and explains why it can be transported in nothing more than a wet sack. The scales are large, numbering from 34 to 40 along the lateral line, with 5-6 rows above and 5-6 rows below it. Breeding has thrown up some sports, i.e. genetic deviations from type, among the normally scaled or king carp, however, and such deviants can occur even in the wild. 'Leather' carp are practically devoid of scales, and 'mirror' carp have only a few much enlarged scales carried in only one or two rows on each side, usually near the back, head or tail.

Breeding takes place in springtime when water temperature has risen to at least 61° F (16° C). As with other cyprinids, the male carp then have small white nuptial nodules around their heads. Two or three males may sometimes be seen in weedy shallows, chasing a female, to the accompaniment of noisy splashes. Female carp are prolific, depositing on the shallow bottom and on the fronds of water plants more than 60,000 eggs per pound of body-weight, so a 10 lb (4.5 kg) carp may lay about 650,000 eggs per season and repeat this for many years. The eggs are 1/16th inch (1.5 mm) in diameter and hatch in about four days to larval fish a quarter-inch (6 mm) long, having a yolk-sac attached that provides nourishment for about a week, by which time a growing fish can find plant and animal foods for itself. Common carp reach sexual maturity at three or four years and may live for up to 40 years, during which time they will continue to grow if food is plentiful.

The food of common carp is partly vegetable (green algae such as silkweed, and the leaves of small water plants) and partly animal (worms, insects and their larvae, freshwater shrimps and slaters). Foraging on the bottom with the aid of their four barbels and extensible mouth, carp will suck in palatable mud and presently eject the indigestible particles. Common carp have no teeth in the mouth but three rows of pharyngeal teeth in the throat, arranged 1-1-3 and 3-1-1. The alimentary canal is remarkable in that it has no sac-like stomach. Digestion practically ceases below 40° F (4.5° C) but increases as temperature rises and is at an optimum around 68° F (20° C).

In 1964, the Bristol Avon River Board obtained 100 one-year-old mirror carp of the 'Redmire' strain from the Surrey Trout Farm Ltd. and planted them out in stock ponds at Prior Park, Bath, where they grew, matured and reproduced, in due course providing stocks for distribution to local angling associations that had suitable waters.

The British record rod-caught carp was a mirror type taken in 1952 by Mr. Richard Walker at Redmire Pool in Herefordshire; it weighed 44 lb (19.957 kg). This is reported to have been exceeded in 1980 by one of 51 lb 8 oz (23.360 kg) caught, again at Redmire Pool, by Mr. C. Yates. In the Bristol Avon catchment the common carp record for the Kennet & Avon Canal has stood for some years at 14 lb 4 oz 4 drm (6.471 kg); a common carp of 15 lb 15 oz 12 drm (7.250 kg) was taken in 1969 by Mr. R. Songhurst at Longleat, and a typical river carp of 16 lb 5 oz 0 drm (7.399 kg) was taken in 1973 by Mr. M. Ainger on the Avon at Hanham. These local records have since been broken by what appear to be the progeny of the River Board's 1964 acquisitions. In July 1974, a Mr. Ganke took a mirror carp of 19 lb 13 oz 4 drm (8.994 kg) from Silverlands Lake, near Lacock; this was immediately exceeded by a mirror carp of 19 lb 13 oz 8 drm (9.001 kg) taken by

Fig. 23 Mirror carp, Cyprinus carpio *cultivar. The cultivation of common carp over many centuries has evolved some remarkable kinds that will breed more or less true to type. These include leather carp, which have practically no scales, and mirror carp, which have only a few irregularly distributed large scales*

Mr. I. Pulsford from Bitterwell Lake, near Bristol. The river record was broken in 1984 by Mr. T. Sullivan, who took a mirror carp of 17 lb 12 oz 0 drm (8.051 kg) from the Avon near Willsbridge.

Crucian Carp and Goldfish

Like the common carp, the crucian carp is not a native British fish but came originally from Asia and has been widely cultivated in ponds for many centuries. The word 'crucian' is a corruption of *Karausche*, the German name for this fish. In appearance and habits a crucian carp resembles a small common carp, but the relationship is sufficiently distant to place it in another genus, and it is known to science as *Carassius carassius*. There is only one row of pharyngeal teeth, for instance, placed four on each side of the throat, in contrast with three rows in the common carp. The dorsal fin, though long (the branched rays numbering 14-21), is slightly rounded, the tail fin is scarcely forked but rather concave, and very distinctively there are no barbels. Scales counted along the lateral line number 34-40 in normally scaled common carp, 28-35 in crucian carp and 25-30 in goldfish. Crucian carp have seldom been known to exceed 4 or 5 lb (2 kg) in weight, the largest on record being one of 5 lb 10 oz 8 drm (2.566 kg) caught in 1976 by Mr. G. Halls at King's Lynn.

In the Bristol Avon catchment, crucian carp may be found in the Kennet & Avon Canal and in a few small lakes such as at Emborough (Lechmere), Witham Friary

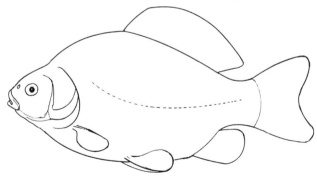

Fig. 24 Crucian carp, Carassius carassius

64

and Lacock (Silverlands). There used to be crucian carp in the lowest stretch of the River Boyd, derived from the mill-pond of the one-time Golden Valley Paper Mill at Bitton; their descendants may still be in the vicinity. The area record for a crucian carp is 3 lb 11 oz 0 drm (1.673 kg), taken in 1985 by Mr. L. Allison at Bowood Lake, near Calne.

Uncertainty attaches to the status of goldfish and Prussian carp, both of which may have evolved in the breeding of crucian carp; some authorities call the goldfish a species and the Prussian carp a sub-species, with the names *Carassius auratus* and *Carassius auratus gibelio* respectively. Although not found naturally in rivers, goldfish are commonly stocked in aquaria and garden pools, from which they might escape or be discarded into a local brook. The distinctive coloration of goldfish may not persist in the wild state, being replaced by olive-green or brown, but goldfish strains can be distinguished by the presence of one or more strong sawtooth spines at the commencement of the long dorsal fin, as in the common carp. Goldfish have no barbels. The number of scales on a goldfish from the leading edge of the dorsal fin down to the lateral line is 5-6½; on a crucian carp it is 6½-9.

Barbel

The barbel (*Barbus barbus*) is a species native to the eastern rivers of England which in prehistoric times were part of the Rhine drainage system. It was not present in the Bristol Avon or its tributaries until 1955, when with the practical cooperation of *Angling Times* journalists, led by Mr. Peter Tombleson (later Executive Director of the National Anglers' Council), Bath Anglers' Association and the Bristol Avon River Board, 52 barbel, electrically fished from a tributary of the River Kennet, were planted into the Avon just downstream of Limpley Stoke. These fish have bred and have been supplemented here and elsewhere in the Bristol Avon by further plantings from the same vicinity. In 1969 and the early 1970s, a fair degree of success attended Michael Amey, at that time Fisheries Superintendent for the Bristol Avon River Authority, in artificially stripping ripe barbel and inseminating and incubating their eggs. Avon barbel have penetrated into some of the tributaries, so today barbel may be expected wherever there are strong flows of water over clean gravels, as happens at the downstream end of most weir pools.

The barbel is a long and muscular olive-green fish. As befits a bottom feeder, its crescent-shaped mouth is set well back below the prominent snout and is equipped with four barbels (rarely five or six). The dorsal fin, positioned midway along the back, is short, having 3-4 hard spines and only 8-9 branched rays. The scales are rather small, numbering 56-60 (extremely 52-70) along the lateral line. Young barbel may be confused with gudgeon or loach; no spines may be detectable in the dorsal fin and all three are likely to have various marks along the flanks and on the finnage. They may be distinguished, however, by the numbers of barbels or wattles around the mouth: gudgeon 2, barbel 4, loach 6.

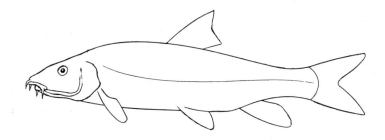

Fig. 25 Barbel, Barbus barbus

Barbel spawn relatively late, about the end of May, when water temperature has reached 63° F (17° C). A 2 lb (1 kg) female lays about 9,000 transparent yellowish eggs, 2 mm in diameter, on a hollow in the gravel, larger fish proportionately more; males add their milt, and the female covers the eggs with more gravel. The eggs hatch in about ten days; the yolk-sac is quickly absorbed and the young barbel grow rapidly on a diet of diatoms, unicellular algae and small insect larvae. As they become bigger they feed mostly by night, prospecting on the river bottom for vegetable particles, worms, freshwater slaters and shrimps, water snails, insect larvae and unconsidered trifles such as

66

anglers' ground-bait. The bigger fish also take fish fry. Barbel are known to have reached at least 14 years of age.

When barbel were introduced to the Bristol Avon, the River Authority placed a restriction on their removal but allowed fishing with rod and line; a new byelaw now forbids the permanent removal of any coarse fish except pike and eels without the prior written consent of the Water Authority. A specimen barbel may be kept alive in a large keep-net or suitable container until verified. The present record for the largest rod-caught barbel on the Bristol Avon is 12 lb 8 oz 0 drm (5.670 kg) for one taken in 1986 by Mr. Michael Stevens near Chippenham. The River Marden has twice provided sub-area records, the latest a barbel of 7 lb 8 oz 12 drm (3.423 kg).

Gudgeon

The gudgeon (*Gobio gobio*), with its long body, prominent snout and forked tail, may be said to look like a miniature barbel. However, the gudgeon has only two barbels (wattles), not four; and along its indeterminately tinted flanks, just above the lateral line, are evenly distributed about a dozen bluish 'finger marks' of rectangular shape. As with barbel, the tail fin is well forked. The gudgeon is a small fish, however, not known to exceed 10 inches (25 cm) in length or 10½ ounces (0.3 kg) in weight, usually attaining a length of no more than 6 inches (15 cm); the British rod-caught record is only 4 oz 4 drm (0.120 kg).

Details of gudgeon are variable, and at one time the species was split up into several sub-species based on dimensions and coloration. It may be said that the single dorsal fin is short, having 0-3 unbranched and 6-8 branched rays. The scales are fairly large, numbering 39-45 along the lateral line, 5-6 from the front of the dorsal fin down to the lateral line, and about 4 from the lateral line down to the leading corner of the ventral fin.

As is the way with small fish, gudgeon go about in shoals, usually in shallow water and foraging on the bottom for vegetable debris and filamentous algae, and for small crustaceans, small water snails and particularly chironomid and other insect larvae, which form at least half of their diet. They are also food for predatory fish and water birds.

Spawning commences in May and may go on into the summer. As is usual with cyprinids, the males develop white nuptial nodules around their heads. A female lays her eggs in running water, not a large number at a time but possibly up to 3,000 in a season; they are small, transparent and adhesive, staying in small clumps on the river bottom. Not all are fertilized by the males and there is much predation by other fish and invertebrate animals such as dragonfly nymphs. Incubation takes about ten days, and the larval fish that emerge have a very large yolk-sac to sustain them until they can support themselves on diatoms and unicellular algae, and in due course larger organisms.

Gudgeon are found in most of the rivers and streams of the Bristol Avon system as well as in lakes and ponds and the Kennet & Avon Canal. No local record has been established yet: a gudgeon of 6¼ inches (15.9 cm) in length and weighing 3 ounces (0.085 kg) was caught in 1980 on the River Marden but could not be accepted as a record specimen because it was spawn-bound and dropsical.

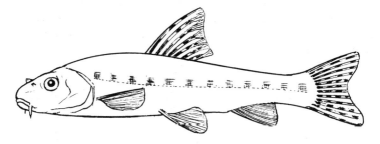

Fig. 26 Gudgeon, Gobio gobio

Minnow

The minnow (*Phoxinus phoxinus*) is smaller than the gudgeon, seldom exceeding 4 inches (10 cm) from snout to fork of the tail. It has a cylindrical body, fairly deep in the belly but long in the wrist of the tail. The general colour is green, but a minnow is whitish beneath, has a narrow golden stripe running along each side, and there are some dark vertical streaks descending from the back towards the flanks. The single dorsal fin is short, having only 3 unbranched and 7 branched rays. The scales are very small

68

and numerous, from 80 to 100 along the lateral line. The tubules in scales along the lateral line extend right across the exposed surface, but the lateral line sometimes peters out before reaching the tail. Distinction from gudgeon and loach can be inferred from the minnow's lack of barbels (gudgeon have 2 barbels, loach 6), from the narrow golden band running along each flank, and from the dark vertical bars that reach down from the back.

In April, as the spawning season approaches, the males become darker but more colourful, the lips, belly and paired fins taking on a scarlet hue while conspicuous whitish nuptial nodules appear around the head. Spawning proceeds in May and June over gravel beds, the female shedding about a thousand tiny eggs that adhere to stones and water plants.

Minnows prefer clear, shallow, well-oxygenated running water and are found in shoals throughout the Bristol Avon river system wherever this condition is satisfied, particularly in the hill streams. They feed on algae, small worms, the larvae of mosquitoes and other insects, small crustaceans and the eggs of other fish. In turn they contribute substantially to the food of predatory fish, especially the larger trout, and of water birds.

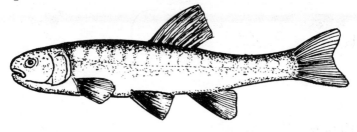

Fig. 27 Minnow, Phoxinus phoxinus

Tench

The tench (*Tinca tinca*) has been described as the most sluggish of our freshwater fishes. It can live in the dirtiest of water at very low oxygen concentrations, even down to less than 10% saturation value, and will survive in the mud of a pond when drought prevails and visible water has

69

evaporated. Tench are to be found in nearly all the slower waters of the Bristol Avon and its major tributaries, in the Kennet & Avon Canal, in the Bristol Floating Harbour and Feeder Canal, and in ponds and old lakes that have gone eutrophic.

The body of a tench is rather stout, oval in cross-section, flattish along the belly but slightly humped on the back. All the fins are rounded, even the lobes of the shallowly forked tail. The dorsal fin is short, having only 3-4 un-branched and 8-9 branched rays. On approaching sexual maturity the males undergo a strengthening and lengthening of the paired ventral fins, particularly of the second ray thereof, so that if laid right back each fin can reach the anal orifice. The mouth is down-turned and at each corner a barbel hangs from the upper lip. The scales are very small, about a hundred along the lateral line, which curves behind the gill-cover but is otherwise nearly straight. The general coloration is green, dark on the back but yellower on the belly. Golden tench are sometimes encountered in the Avon; these are sports, believed to have a genetic irregularity that affects their production of melanin, the black pigment, so that the scales are pigmented only by carotene (red) and xanthophyll (yellow).

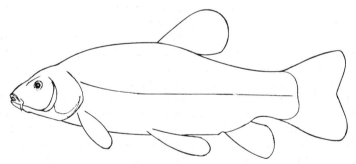

Fig. 28 Tench, Tinca tinca

Tench do not spawn until spring sunshine has warmed the water to about 66° F (19° C), which does not usually happen until June or even July in this river basin, and in a cold summer may not occur at all, so that no spawning takes place and a year class of tench is missed. In a normal year, however, a female tench produces about 100,000 eggs per pound of body-weight, which she sheds in batches in weedy shallows, a male or males being in attendance to shed milt. The eggs are 1.5 mm in diameter and adhere to weeds, hatching in about a week if the temperature is maintained, whereupon larval tench emerge complete with yolk-sac and start to grow rapidly, soon foraging for diatoms, unicellular algae, protozoans, water-fleas and other small plankton. The food of larger tench consists of organic debris extracted from mud, together with water weeds, worms, insects and their larvae, water slaters and pulmonate snails, mostly foraged for at night with the aid of the two barbels.

In the Bristol Avon catchment the largest rod-caught tench on record is one of 7 lb 6 oz (3.345 kg) taken in 1941 by Mr. J. F. Butler in Duchess Pond, Stapleton (since drained). The Bristol Avon itself has yielded a tench of 6 lb 3 oz (2.807 kg) and the Kennet & Avon Canal one of 5 lb 12 oz (2.608 kg).

Roach

In terms of aggregate mass of fish, the most successful species in the Bristol Avon catchment is undoubtedly the roach (*Rutilus rutilus*), which is found throughout in nearly all rivers, lakes, ponds, stretches of canal and even dock basins. Such universality indicates a wide tolerance in variables such as water temperature, pH (hydrogen-ion concentration, a measure of alkalinity and acidity), dissolved oxygen, mineral content, depth, water speed, and availability of food organisms, while at the same time reflecting the consistency of local waters. Roach diet is a mixed one that includes a large proportion of unicellular and filamentous algae and small water plants, and smaller quantities of crustaceans (water-fleas, slaters and shrimps), insects and their nymphs, and water snails. Spawning takes place in late May and June at a water temperature of at least 64° F (18° C), which scarcely ever fails to happen, and a 2 lb (1 kg) female lays as many as 100,000 tiny eggs, so there is every chance of keeping filled what is undoubtedly a favourable ecological niche. In gravel pits, roach tend to multiply but become stunted for lack of adequate natural foods. Once they have survived to adulthood, roach usually

71

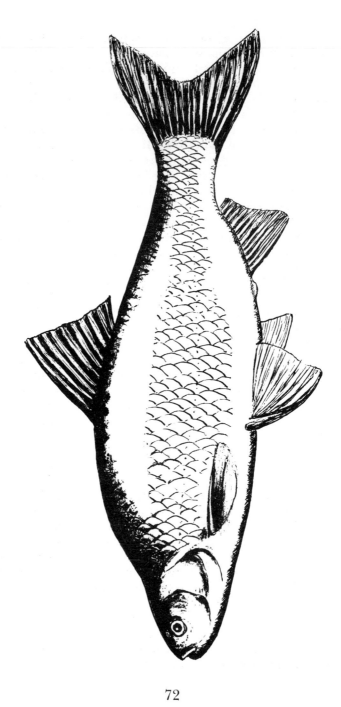

Fig. 29 Roach, Rutilus rutilus

live for eight, nine or ten years, but they are believed to have a maximum life of 18 years. The feeding pattern of roach is compared with that of common bream in the table on page 80.

Well-grown river roach are beautiful silvery fish with tails and dorsal fins coloured orange and grey, ventral (pelvic) and anal fins suffused with red, and an unmistakable red iris around the pupil of each eye. The body is evenly scaled, having 40-46 scales along the gently curving lateral line. The dorsal fin is characteristic; it is concave and short, having 3 hard and 9-11 branched soft rays, and its leading edge is positioned midway along the back in line with those of the ventral fins. The anal fin also is concave and short. The upper lip projects slightly, so in effect the mouth is just below the snout.

The largest roach taken locally by rod and line is, to date, one of 2 lb 12 oz (1.247 kg) caught in 1948 by Mr. H. C. Lowe in Chew Magna Reservoir. The record for the Bristol Avon is 2 lb 5 oz 8 drm (1.063 kg) and for the Somerset Frome 2 lb 5 oz 4 drm (1.056 kg).

Black spots with a slightly raised centre may sometimes be seen in the skin of roach and less often other freshwater fish. These are caused by the larvae of a trematode (i.e. a parasitic flatworm or 'fluke') named *Neodiplostomum cuticola* that are picked up from the surrounding water, penetrate the fish's protective mucous covering and encyst under the epidermis. If an affected fish is eaten by a water bird the encysted flukes are liberated by digestive juices, mature to adult flukes in the warm intestine and proceed to mate and produce eggs that are soon voided in the droppings. When dropped into water an egg hatches into a swimming 'first larva' that promptly finds and enters the body of a water snail. There it multiplies asexually, eventually producing a second type of larvae that may themselves have daughter larvae; these develop into yet a third type of larvae that break out of the snail, swim freely and latch on to a fish, thus starting the cycle over again. 'Black spot' is not confined to the Bristol Avon catchment, but fish in slow or still waters such as the Kennet & Avon Canal are most easily set upon. The eye fluke *Diplostomum spathaceum* or *volvens*, which causes blindness in cyprinid fish, sticklebacks and rainbow trout, has a similar life-cycle.

Rudd

The rudd (*Scardinius erythrophthalmus*) is an even more colourful fish than the roach, for its ventral, anal and tail fins are crimson; but the iris around each eye is yellow, not red. It resembles the roach, but is slightly deeper in the body, does not grow so big, has a slightly projecting *lower* lip, and its dorsal fin (2-3 hard and 8-9 soft rays) is placed farther back, where the arch of the back begins to fall away towards the tail; a vertical line drawn downwards from the leading edge of the dorsal fin would fall just behind the ventral fins. The scales are large, numbering 39-44 along the lateral line (in contrast with 40-46 on the roach and 49-56 on the common bream). The overall colour of the body is a brassy yellow, but it fades after death.

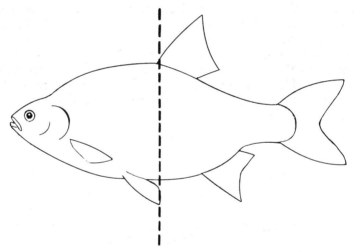

Fig. 30 Rudd, Scardinius erythrophthalmus. *The dorsal fin is set farther back than on the roach*

Rudd do not favour fast-running water, but are to be found sparsely in the Bristol Avon and the larger tributaries, usually near the banks or on weedy bottoms, where they find a diet similar to that of roach, half vegetable and half invertebrate-animal, according to what is available. Some of the lakes and ponds in the south of the Bristol Avon catchment hold rudd that have been introduced there from the lake at Stourhead, and this is probably where the rudd in the Kennet & Avon Canal originally came from. Rudd spawn in a similar way to roach and other cyprinids, but they need a water temperature of about 68° F (20° C), which means they spawn late in the springtime and in a cold season might miss a year.

The local record for a rod-caught rudd is one of 10 oz (0.283 kg) taken in 1964 by Mr. R. J. Cox from the Somerset Frome, but it is probable that there are larger rudd to be taken.

Dace

The dace (*Leuciscus leuciscus*) is like a roach, but smaller, noticeably slimmer and less highly coloured, the general coloration being a silvery green-blue, darker on the back, paler on the belly, with a slight reddish tinge in the grey finnage. The tail fin makes a straight-cut fork. A characteristic feature is the narrow dorsal fin (3 hard and 7-8 branched rays), positioned midway along the back and in line with the ventral fins, its outer edge being distinctly concave. The anal fin (3 hard and 7-9 branched rays) also is concave. The scales are neat, usually 47-54 along the lateral line, but rarely 45-55.

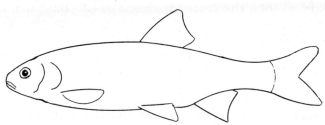

Fig. 31 Dace, Leuciscus leuciscus. *The trailing edges of the dorsal and anal fins are 'dented', in contrast with those of the chub*

In marked contrast with tench, dace are the liveliest and daintiest of the carp family. Naturally shy and cautious, they demand an angler's finest tackle and all his skill. Dace like swiftly moving water, and may be found throughout the Avon and its major tributaries wherever there are fast shallows or strong flows below a weir. Usually they congregate in shoals.

Spawning takes place in a manner similar to that of other cyprinid fishes already described. It happens in April and May, a water temperature of 61° F (16° C) being sufficient. The males develop the usual nuptial nodules before the event, and when it is over, both sexes seek the bubbling, well-oxygenated water below a weir in which to recover. Diatoms figure very large in the diet of young dace, so do unicellular algae; but as they grow, dace take an increasing interest in insect larvae, and when they have reached a size of about 4 inches (10 cm) at two years of age, their diet is half made up of insects in all stages of their life-cycles, many of them seized at the water surface. The other half of their diet consists of filamentous algae (silkweed), crustaceans such as freshwater shrimps and slaters, and water snails of the smaller sizes.

The largest rod-caught dace on record for the Bristol Avon catchment is one of 14 oz 4 drm (0.404 kg) caught in 1976 by Mr. M. Lewis in the By Brook at Box. The present record for the Bristol Avon itself is 13 oz (0.369 kg).

Chub

The chub (*Leuciscus cephalus*) somewhat resembles both the roach and the dace, but its body is less deep and more cylindrical than the roach. Its large mouth has thick lips, and all its outlines are rounded. In particular the dorsal fin (3 hard and 8-9 branched rays), positioned midway along the back as on roach and dace, is convex along its outer edge; the outline of the anal fin is even more rounded. On the dace these fins are concave, hence the anglers' mnemonic: 'curved chub and dented dace'. The general coloration is a silvery amethyst; the large eyes have a golden iris; the paired ventral fins and the anal fin are orange-red. The large scales are dark at the base, numbering 44-46 along the lateral line (compared with 40-46 on roach, 47-54 on dace).

Chub are found in the faster-flowing stretches of the Bristol Avon and its major tributaries, young chub in shoals, older fish solitary near a gravelly bottom but always close to a cavernous or weedy refuge. Spawning takes place early in the spring, from April onwards, a water temperature of 59° F (15° C) being adequate. Prior to spawning,

76

nuptial nodules appear around the heads of the males and the fins glow brighter. A male matures at two years, a female at three. According to size, a female lays between 50,000 and 100,000 eggs, 1.5 mm in diameter, which adhere to water plants, twigs, roots and stones. They hatch in about a week, and while the yolk-sac is being absorbed, the larval fish learn to feed on diatoms, which are common at that time of year before the burst of invertebrate activity. Algae, buds of water plants and other vegetable matter continue to play a large part in the diet of chub, but a taste develops early for insect larvae and crustaceans, and as the summer progresses and the chub grows, adult insects at the water surface are sought, as befits a surface-swimming fish with a big up-turned mouth. Animal food plays an increasing part in the diet as the chub matures, and older chub are credited with eating crayfish, snails, frogs and fish fry, as well as seeds and berries that might drop into the water. As with so many other fish that lay large numbers of eggs and produce shoals of offspring, predation on chub is heavy and along with other cyprinids they are prey for pike, perch and water birds.

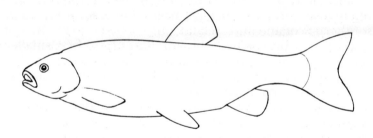

Fig. 32 Chub, Leuciscus cephalus. *The trailing edges of the dorsal and anal fins are 'curved', in contrast with those of the dace*

The largest rod-caught chub on record for the Bristol Avon is one of 7 lb 5 oz 2 drm (3.320 kg) taken in 1986 by Master Paul J. Goddard (aged 14 years) at Peckingell, which comes near the British record of 7 lb 6 oz (3.345 kg). The Somerset Frome has yielded a chub of 3 lb 15 oz (1.786 kg), the Chew one of 2 lb 8 oz (1.134 kg) and the Marden one of 2 lb 0 oz (0.907 kg).

77

Golden Orfe

Although the orfe or ide (*Leuciscus idus*) is a close relative of the dace and the chub, it is not a British fish and is not found wild in the Bristol Avon catchment. However, it sometimes sports a golden form, from which Continental fish breeders have raised stock and which from 1874 onwards has been imported into the United Kingdom for display in ornamental pools, as at Oakhill Manor. A golden orfe of 3 lb 14 oz 8 drm (1.772 kg) caught in September 1973 by Mr. D. Stevens in the Winford Brook at Chew Magna is assumed to have been washed out of such a pool in the phenomenal flood there of 10th-11th July 1968; it set up both a local and (for a time) a British rod-caught record, but the latter has moved on to 4 lb 3 oz 8 drm (1.914 kg) for a golden orfe caught in 1983 by Mr. D. R. Charles in the River Kennet. Golden orfe raised by Mr. V. Alder in 1962 for his garden pool at Bath attained weights between 2 and 3 lb (1-1.4 kg) and lived for 20 years.

Bream

The common or bronze bream (*Abramis brama*) is a Continental species long since naturalized in eastern England, southern Scotland and Ireland, but not native to the Bristol Avon. The white or silver bream, *Blicca bjoernka,* a smaller relative, is common on the Continent but rare and local in Britain, being found in the wild only in the eastern counties of England from Suffolk to Yorkshire, and absent from the Bristol Avon. However, in 1903, the Bath Anglers' Association planted a consignment of young silver bream from the eastern counties into the Avon upstream of Bathampton Weir; two were caught about a year later weighing 1¾ lb (0.8 kg) and 3 lb (1.4 kg). These weights are heavy for typical silver bream, and one wonders whether the planted fish were really silver bream or were probably common bream, the young of both species being practically indistinguishable. Interest re-awakened in the early 1920s when the Avon Preservation & Restocking Society successfully introduced common bream from East Anglia into the Somerset Axe, and from there in 1923 transferred a stock to the Bristol Avon. This early stock has been reinforced from time to time by further plantings, so that today stocks of common bream are well established in the deeper and slower parts of the Avon, from the Bristol Floating Harbour as far up as Dauntsey, also in the lower stretches of the Chew, Boyd, By Brook, Midford Brook, Somerset Frome, Biss and Semington Brook, and in the Kennet & Avon Canal. The common bream grows quickly into a big fish, but when hooked offers little resistance. It is therefore a popular quarry with competition anglers, in spite of its exorbitant demands for ground-bait to attract it and keep it on the feed in a given swim. The record 5 hour all-in competition top individual weight for the Bristol Avon, achieved in 1985 by Mr. M. G. Haskins at Swineford with 114 lb 3 oz (51.794 kg), was almost exclusively common bream, and the 5½ hour competition weight of Mr. F. Coe on the Avon at Chippenham the same year, namely 146 lb 9 oz (66.480 kg), consisted solely of 35 bream, the heaviest weighing 7 lb 15 oz (3.600 kg).

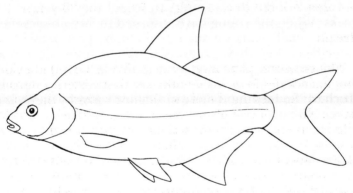

Fig. 33 Common bream, Abramis brama

In silhouette the common bream presents a fine figure of a fish, portly but not quite stately because the head is rather small for a big fish; seen end-on or from above, the bream is disappointingly narrow, earning for itself derisive titles such as 'bellows' and 'dinner plate'. The young are silvery, with pale fins; but adult bream, a foot (30 cm) or more in length, are pale brown in colour, with a bronzy sheen that disappears after death, and the fins are dark grey. The dorsal fin is short (3 hard and 8-10 branched

79

rays), but the anal fin is long (3 hard and 23-30 branched rays), running upwards from the belly towards the tail at an angle of 30° from the horizontal. The tail fin is widely forked, its lower lobe longer than the upper. There are no barbels. The scales are large and regular, 51-56 (extremely 49-60) along the lateral line and 11-15 from the leading corner of the dorsal fin down to the lateral line. (The silver bream, unlikely to be found in the Bristol Avon, has 43-50 scales along the lateral line and 8-11 from dorsal fin to lateral line.) The breast and belly are devoid of scales.

Bream congregate to spawn in shoals, at intervals during May and June, on weedy shallows where the water has been warmed up by spring sunshine to 64° F (18° C). Nuptial nodules on the males extend from head to back, and smaller ones may be seen on the finnage. Oldest fish tend to spawn earliest. A female bream lays about 100,000 eggs per pound of body-weight, say 200,000-500,000 in a season; they are pale yellow, about 1.5 millimetres in diameter, and they adhere to water plants, where they hatch in 1-3 weeks. When the young have absorbed their yolk-sacs they live on small plankton such as diatoms, protozoans and water-fleas, but they progress to filamentous algae and portions of water plants and to small animal life found on the bottom, including worms, insect larvae, water slaters and snails. Much of the feeding is done in shallow water by night, but by day bream prospect in deep water, stirring the mud with their projecting snouts. The items of diet are similar to those of roach, and it might be expected that roach and bream would be in competition, perhaps to the detriment of the native roach; but according to the Freshwater Biological Association's survey of the food of coarse fishes, conducted in East Anglia, the proportions are very different:

Percentage Frequency of Occurrences in Fish Stomachs (Not by weight)

	Common Bream	Roach
Unicellular algae and diatoms	2	12
Filamentous algae and larger plants	23	55
Insects and their larvae	20	11
Crustaceans	51	14
Molluscs	4	8
Small fish	Nil	Nil

In all but the close season for coarse fish, any such figures would need adjustment for the vast quantities of maggots and other ground-bait for which bream are privileged recipients. The locations of bream and roach are seldom identical, and it would seem that each has its ecological niche.

The present record for a rod-caught bream in the Bristol Avon is 8 lb 8 oz (3.856 kg) taken in 1965 by Mr. W. F. Matthews at Chippenham. The Kennet & Avon Canal has produced a bream of 7 lb 1 oz (3.204 kg).

Bleak

The bleak (*Alburnus alburnus*) is a dainty little fish, about 6 inches (15 cm) long, that goes about in shoals in slowly moving water, usually shallow. Its distribution in England and Wales is irregular, and there is a tradition that it is not native to the Bristol Avon but was brought from the Thames catchment as live-bait for pike. It is widespread now, from Bristol at least as far up as Dauntsey, and as it is a prolific spawner at a time when other members of the carp family are similarly engaged, hybridizing is not uncommon.

Bleak have a slender body, much narrowed at the wrist of the tail (but nothing like as much as in the stickleback), and the overall colour is silvery-green, lighter below and darker on the back. The mouth is noticeably oblique, almost vertical, the lip on the lower jaw coming up to project beyond the upper jaw. The dorsal fin (3-4 hard and 7-9 branched rays) is rounded and set farther back than an imaginary vertical line drawn across the middle of the fish, while the paired ventral (pelvic) fins are just forward of

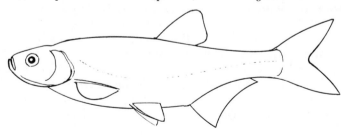

Fig. 34 Bleak, Alburnus alburnus

such a line. The anal fin, however, is bream-like, being concave and long from front to back, with 3 hard and 15-19 branched rays. The scales number 42-52 along the lateral line, and over the belly they form a sharp keel.

Bleak spawn in April and May in a manner very much like that of the other cyprinids, and their offspring feed on plankton, small organisms at first but gradually progressing to larger morsels such as chironomid larvae, waterfleas and small flies at the surface. In turn they are food for bigger fish and for water birds.

A bleak of 2 oz 0 drm (0.057 kg) was taken in 1982 by Mr. A. Ponting on the Bristol Avon at Chippenham.

Hybrids

Cross-breeding within the carp family is not uncommon, and as may be expected the offspring usually show characteristics intermediate between those of the parents, but with a possible bias toward one or the other. The following are some hybrids that are likely to be encountered in the Bristol Avon catchment.

Carp × *crucian carp*, possible in the Kennet & Avon Canal and lakes such as Silverlands. The dorsal fin is straight and long, with 3-4 hard and 14-21 branched rays as in the parents. There may be two pairs of barbels with the upper pair very small or there may be barbels only at each corner of the mouth (cp. common carp two pairs, crucian carp nil). The cleft of the tail fin is wide rather than deep. Scales in the lateral line number 33-38 (cp. common carp 34-40, crucian carp 28-35).

Roach × *rudd*, likely to be found in the Somerset Frome, lakes in the vicinity of Frome and in the Kennet & Avon Canal; difficult to detect because of the similarity of the parents. The ventral, anal and tail fins may be of a brighter red than on a roach, and the iris of the eye may be red as in roach rather than yellow as in rudd. The scales are large, 42-43 along the lateral line (cp. roach 40-46, rudd 39-44). The leading corner of the dorsal fin is vertically above the middle of the ventral fins. The mouth is terminal (cp. upper lip projects on roach, lower lip projects on rudd).

Roach × *bream*, a very common hybrid, often mistaken for a big roach. There are 47-52 scales along the lateral line (cp. roach 40-46, bream 49-56, occasionally more), and the number from the leading corner of the dorsal fin diagonally down to the lateral line is about 10 (cp. roach 8-9, bream 11-15); from the lateral line down to the leading corner of the ventral fins 5-6 (cp. roach 3-4½, bream 6-7). The anal fin is longer than on roach, having 15-19 branched rays (cp. roach 9-12, bream 23-30).

Roach × bleak, could be mistaken for a specimen bleak. The branched rays in the anal fin are about 15 in number (cp. roach 9-12, bleak 15-19). Other distinctions from a true bleak are orange or red coloration in the finnage and the iris of the eye, and a greater depth of body, especially noticeable in a marked rounding of the back. A distinction from pure roach is a keel-like ridge along the belly.

Bleak hybrids with roach or any other cyprinid have the dorsal fin well behind the level of the ventral fins. The length and shape of the dorsal and anal fins should always be observed.

Dace hybrids can be difficult, and confusion between dace and chub is always possible. The dorsal and anal fins of chub are rounded in outline ('curved chub'); those of the dace are squarish at the corners and concave along the trailing edge ('dented dace').

11. Loaches

The loach family (Cobitidae) are not far removed from the carp family, sharing many of their characteristics, such as the single dorsal fin, numerous branched fin rays, absence of teeth in the mouth and presence of pharyngeal teeth in the throat. They differ in the numbers and arrangement of the pharyngeal teeth (in loaches there are from 8 to 14, arranged in a single row), the numbers of barbels, the shapes of the tail fins and in some internal details. Loaches have a remarkable facility for surviving low dissolved-oxygen or dried-up conditions by gulping atmospheric air down into the intestine, later passing it out by way of the anus with less oxygen and more carbon dioxide.

Of the two British species of loach, only one, the common or stone loach (*Nemacheilus barbatulus*, previously called *Cobitis barbatula*), is known with certainty to inhabit the Bristol Avon catchment, where it is found frequently in still or running water having a bottom of stones under which it can take shelter. The beds of sandstone over which the Bristol Frome flows and the plates of limestone in streams coming off the Cotswolds or the Mendips provide just such a habitat. Stone loaches rarely exceed 4 inches (10 cm) in length. They have long, spindly bodies of a dull yellow-ochre colour mottled with sepia in large and small patches. The head is compressed vertically, the upper lip projects over the mouth, and very distinctively there are six barbels: two small pairs above the mouth and a long barbel at each corner of the mouth. The fins are evenly distributed, the dorsal being placed in the middle of the back; they all bear some dark vertical bars or vestigial speckles. The tail fin is not divided but is a single fluke, fairly

Fig. 35 Stone loach, Nemacheilus barbatulus

wide and rounded off at the corners. The scales are very small indeed and lie side by side without overlapping.

Stone loaches breed in late spring and early summer. They feed on microscopic bottom-living animals and are themselves prey for other fishes and any other carnivorous animals around the waterside. If not eaten prematurely, a stone loach may live for five or six years.

It is just possible that the spined loach or groundling (*Cobitis taenia*), found in eastern England, may be lurking undiscovered in some of our waters. In general appearance it is like the stone loach, and differences may be appreciated only if both species can be laid side by side. It is smaller, however, seldom more than 3 inches (7½ cm) long; the blotches on the sides form a regular chain pattern; all six barbels are equally long; and there are two tiny spines lying in a hollow below the eyes that are hard enough to prick a finger. If spined loaches do inhabit local waters they may easily hitherto have been mistaken for stone loach. Here is an opportunity for an original investigation.

Fig. 36 Perch, Perca fluviatilis

12. The Perch Family

Characteristic features of the perch family (Percidae) are the two large dorsal fins, the more forward of which is stiffened by hard spines, and the position of the pair of ventral fins (more properly here called the pelvic fins) vertically beneath the pair of pectoral fins. In some species the two dorsal fins are continuous, but in such a case the anterior portion is made up of large hard spines and the posterior mostly of softer and branched rays. Percid scales are tough, rough, sometimes spiny, and they are ctenoid in plan view, i.e. they have a comb-like edge.

Perch

The perch (*Perca fluviatilis*) is a freshwater member of the perch family but is tolerant of brackish water; it prefers slowly running water with plenty of weed or bank cover, but is quite at home in still lakes if they have sun-warmed shallows. Perch are found in small numbers practically throughout the Bristol Avon and its major tributaries, in the Kennet & Avon Canal, in the Bristol Floating Harbour and in most of the larger lakes. It is a distinctive and colourful fish: silvery yellow on the flanks, with about seven vertical stripes descending from the dark-green back; white on the belly; ventral (pelvic), anal and tail fins tinged with deep orange; eyes with a golden iris; two heraldic-looking fins surmounting the back. The two dorsal fins are not quite joined: the foremost (13-17 hard spines) has a black spot at its posterior end and is longer than the other (which has 1-2 smaller spines and 13-15 closely set branched rays). The mouth is large and well provided with teeth. The scales are rough and cover not only the body but the head and gill-covers.

Perch are gregarious fish and they spawn in shoals from early April onwards to August, a water temperature of 50° F (10° C) being sufficient for this purpose. The females criss-cross weed beds with ribbons of jelly containing numerous tiny white eggs, possibly up to 200,000 per fish. These hatch in about eighteen days, and although eggs and young are highly preyed upon the survivors grow rapidly and are soon feeding on small invertebrate animals such as *Cyclops* and *Daphnia*. Adult perch are voracious feeders, and devour other fish as well as fish spawn, insect larvae and pupae, and large crustaceans. Maturity is reached at three years.

The record rod-caught perch for the Bristol Avon catchment is one of 4 lb 11 oz 8 drm (2.140 kg) caught in 1978 by Mr. F. Oatley in one of the lakes at Prior Park, Bath. The largest perch from the Bristol Avon itself, to date, was one of 2 lb 11 oz (1.219 kg).

Ruff

The pope or ruff (*Gymnocephalus cernuus*) is irregularly distributed in the British Isles, but is thought not to be native to the Bristol Avon. It is, however, sometimes found in the upper parts of the river system, to which it might have been brought from the Thames catchment nearby as spawn on the feet of birds; the building of weirs on the Avon may have contributed to the slow and deep water that the ruff favours. This fish is perch-like but smaller and lacking in the bright colours and vertical bar marks of perch. The two dorsal fins coalesce, beginning with 11-16 large spines and then tailing off in 11-15 long but tightly packed branched rays. The pectoral, ventral (pelvic) and widely spread tail fins are well rounded. The general colour

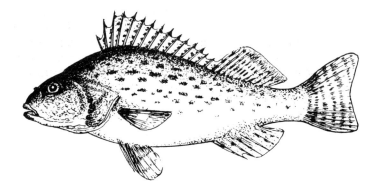

Fig. 37 Ruff, Gymnocephalus cernuus

is a sort of khaki, darkening to grey on the back and paling to beige on the belly; there are large irregular speckles on the body and some dark dashes on the fins with a suggestion of semicircular pattern. The eyes are large and have a mauve iris.

Ruff live mostly on the river bottom, feeding voraciously on worms, insects, insect larvae, water slaters, freshwater shrimps, fish spawn and fry, in fact any small thing that appears to move. Spawning takes place in May, and a female ruff lays some 100,000 tiny eggs in gelatinous strings across weedy shallows; the eggs hatch in 9-14 days. There is no record size for ruff in the Bristol Avon, but 8 inches (20 cm) would be a very big one.

Bass

The bass (*Dicentrarchus labrax*) belongs to the same natural order (Percomorphi) as the freshwater perches but is now grouped in a separate family thereof, the sea perches (Serranidae). Bass are marine fish that come into the Bristol Channel from May to November for spawning purposes and are sometimes carried by tidal movements into the Avon estuary, the Bristol Floating Harbour and possibly the freshwater river. They are perch-like but lack the bright colours and vertical stripes of perch, being instead silvery (as befits a sea fish), bluish along the back and with a dark spot on each gill-cover; young bass ('school bass') have dark speckles on their flanks but the dorsal finnage avoids confusion with sea trout. The foremost of the two dorsal fins has 9 large spines; there is a small gap before the second dorsal fin starts, which comprises about a dozen closely placed rays. A bass might be caught in fishing for sea trout; it should be handled with care because of its sharp spines.

13. Grey Mullets

The grey-mullet family (Mugilidae) contains about 100 species, mostly marine and brackish-water kinds that are found in tropical and Mediterranean places, but three of them visit British coasts in summertime. One of these species is rare, but examples of the other two are likely to be carried from the Bristol Channel into the Avon estuary by tidal movements: they are the thick-lipped grey mullet (*Mugil labrosus*) and the thin-lipped grey mullet (*Mugil ramada*). In recent years the latter has been found in growing numbers on the water-intake screens of Oldbury and Berkeley power stations on the Severn estuary.

The grey mullets all have a broad head and back surmounted by two short dorsal fins, the foremost with four spines, the second placed well back and stiffened with one spine and 8-9 soft rays. The flanks are grey; there is no lateral line but there are several dark-grey lines running horizontally from the head right out to the wide tail fin. The belly is white, sharply demarcated from the grey of the flanks, and the back is a slate blue. The head is scaly, the mouth small and equipped with bristle-like teeth for feeding on seaweeds and bottom debris.

The thick-lipped grey mullet has a thick upper lip with tiny warty nodules. Its pectoral fins are at least three-quarters of the length of the head from snout to rear edge of gill-cover. It can grow to about 10 lb (4½ kg) in weight.

The thin-lipped grey mullet has a thin, smooth upper lip. Its pectoral fins measure less than three-quarters of the length of the head, and above the upper extremity of each pectoral fin is a long and pointed scale looking like a small superficial fin. This species grows to about 5 lb (2¼ kg) in weight.

14. Bullheads

The bullhead family (Cottidae) has four species accredited as British, of which three are marine, the sea-scorpions, and only one, the common bullhead or miller's thumb (*Cottus gobio*), is a freshwater fish. The miller's thumb is found on gravel beds and lurking under stones in most of the clear-running stretches of the Bristol Avon and its tributaries. It rarely exceeds 4 inches (10 cm) in length. Unlike most small fish it is solitary, not gregarious, in its habits. Its very large and vertically compressed head (for which either of its English names is apt) and its pair of large pectoral fins help it to direct water currents so as to hold its place on the stream bottom.

With its oversize head, tapering body and billowy excess of spiny finnage, the miller's thumb looks like the creation of an imaginative heraldic artist. There are two dorsal fins joined by a narrow membrane: the first short and stiffened by 6-9 hard spines, the second long and taller, stiffened by 15-19 rays. The pectoral fins stand out wide and scallop-edged behind expanded gill-covers, and the unremarkable pelvic fins hang closely beneath them. The anal fin is long (10-14 soft spines) and the tail fin spreads like a fan. The skin covering the body bears no scales. Coloration is changeable for defence or attack but basically is olive-brown, with extensive dark-brown mottling on the back and flanks but a lighter shade along the belly. The fin rays are patterned with alternating light and dark bands. The mouth is large and well furnished with small but sharp teeth.

The miller's thumb appears to be lethargic until stimulated to seek prey, whereupon it is quick and almost insatiable. Pairing-off and spawning take place from March onwards, the female depositing her pinkish mass of nearly a thousand eggs in a redd scooped out of the gravel beneath a stone, which the male then guards aggressively for a month during incubation and hatching. As the progeny grow, their diet progresses from minute bottom-living invertebrate animals to larger larvae, insects, freshwater shrimps and slaters, worms, the eggs and fry of other fish, and even minnows or gudgeon as big as themselves.

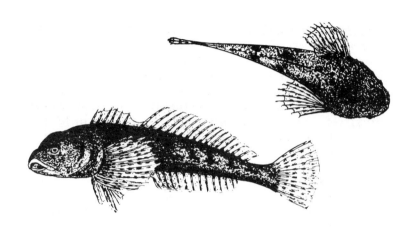

Fig. 38 Bullhead or miller's thumb, Cottus gobio

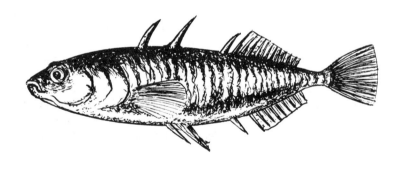

Fig. 39 Three-spined stickleback, Gasterosteus aculeatus

15.   Sticklebacks

The stickleback family (Gasterosteidae) has three British representatives: the fifteen-spined stickleback (*Spinachia spinachia*), a marine species that grows to about 6 inches (15 cm) in length; the nine- or ten-spined stickleback (*Pungitius pungitius*), whose spines vary in number from 8 to 12, which lives in fresh or brackish water irregularly distributed in ponds, ditches and some rivers, and which grows to a length of about 2 inches (5 cm); and the three-spined stickleback (*Gasterosteus aculeatus*) that lives in fresh or brackish water and grows to about 3 inches. The last of these, often called Jack Sharp or tiddler, is the smallest fish found in the Bristol Avon catchment and is widely distributed: in shallows near the banks of rivers and lakes, in the Kennet & Avon Canal, and in semi-tidal dikes and ponds around the Avon estuary.

The three-spined stickleback is almost a caricature of a fish, for although the body is smoothly spindle-shaped, the head, eyes and belly are disproportionately large and the wrist of the tail is as thin as a matchstick, while some of the finnage is reduced to bare spines. There is a neat dorsal fin with 3 hard and 10-12 soft rays set well back near the tail, but in front of it are usually three irregularly spaced strong spines, sometimes four or rarely two. Each of the paired ventral fins is reduced to a strong spine and a soft ray, which lock together as an offensive weapon. There is another spine in front of the neat anal fin. In place of scales the body is more or less protected by little bony plates or shields known as scutes; in cold and saline waters they are numerous, but in temperate fresh waters there are scarcely any, just a few behind the gill-covers, the remainder of the skin being naked and unprotected except for the usual coating of mucus.

The overall colouring of sticklebacks is grey-green, paler beneath, darker above; but from early April until June, the breeding season, the males take on brighter colours, the throat and belly a brilliant red, the flanks horizontally striped and vertically banded with ultramarine, while the females become yellow along the belly. A globular nest is made by binding together strands of weed with gelatinous threads secreted from the male's seasonally swollen kidneys. The female deposits a yellowish pile of eggs through a round hole in the top of the nest, and the male adds his milt, then ferociously mounts guard for the incubation period of about nine days, directing a current of water over eggs and young. The offspring learn to feed on small zooplankton such as *Daphnia* and *Cyclops*, then progress to larger organisms, hunting aggressively for insect larvae, insects, worms, fish spawn and fish fry, indeed every water animal up to their own size. They have also a small intake of green algae. Sticklebacks are themselves a major item of food for trout and other predators.

Sticklebacks in still water are prone to attack by a sporozoan parasite named *Glugea anomala*, which forms large white cysts on the flanks. Inside the cysts are thousands of microscopic spores which are eventually set free and infect more sticklebacks. Sticklebacks are also parasitized by tapeworms of the genus *Schistocephalus*, larval forms of which give the belly a heavily pregnant appearance. An affected stickleback having been eaten by a warm-blooded host such as a grebe, gull or cormorant, the tapeworms come to maturity in the warm gut, where they mate, produce eggs and die. If the eggs are voided into water they yield microscopic larvae that may be eaten by small crustaceans such as *Diaptomus* or *Cyclops*, within which a second larval stage of the parasite develops. If the crustaceans are eaten by a stickleback, a third stage of larvae begins to develop that forces its way through the gut wall and into the body-cavity; then the cycle starts again. Parasitic infestations are quite usual under natural conditions, and most species have their particular pests. Parasites may cause discomfort, but they do not habitually kill their hosts; that is a role falling to predators and to pathogenic bacteria and viruses.

16. The Flounder

The flounder (*Platichthys flesus* or *Pleuronectes flesus*) is an estuarine fish, the only member of the plaice family (Pleuronectidae) that is consistently found in the Avon estuary, the Bristol Floating Harbour, the Feeder Canal and the lower freshwater reaches of the Avon. It penetrates into the latter during the summer, in search of freshwater foods, and swims at least as far up as Keynsham Weir, whose crest is drowned out for only a few minutes at times of high spring tides. In autumn it drops back to salt water, and it is in the vicinity of the Bristol Channel that it spawns between February and May. Flounders' eggs are lighter than sea water and float to the surface, where fertilization with milt takes place; a female of average weight liberates nearly a million eggs less than 1 millimetre in diameter. Incubation takes about a week, according to water temperature, and the larval flounder that emerges from an egg has a yolk-sac on which it subsists for about ten days, after which it feeds on marine diatoms and copepods, progressing ultimately to worms, shrimps and other medium-sized crustaceans, and small shellfish. Predation by other fish and by sea birds is heavy.

A newly hatched flounder is symmetrical, round in cross-section, but at the end of a month it begins to undergo change: the left eye migrates upwards and forwards until it reaches a position above and in front of the right eye; the body depth has meanwhile increased faster than its length and takes on a horizontal position, so the young flounder finally swims and rests on what was initially its left side. Both eyes are by then uppermost and on the right side, and most of the teeth have developed on the under side of the mouth. The under surface of the fish assumes an opaque white, and the upper surface becomes pigmented almost to black. The lateral line that develops is nearly straight. Sometimes a flounder will develop left-sided, that is with its eyes on the left side of the body instead of the right.

Flounders are subject to attack by the sporozoan *Glugea*, which raises white cysts on the surface of the body, as on sticklebacks. They are also set upon by fish 'lice' (really not lice at all but parasitic crustaceans), which cluster on the pectoral fins.

Dabs (a related species, *Limanda limanda*) might be swept into the Avon estuary by tidal movements. They are smaller than flounders, which attain a length of about a foot (30 cm) whereas dabs measure about 8 inches (20 cm). Dabs can be recognized by a semicircular curve in the lateral line above the pectoral fin, a brownish colour and a rough feel to the scales caused by their spiny edges.

17. Fishermen's Flies

Entomology is steeped in Greek and Latin derivations. Winged insects are classified into (*a*) the Exopterygota, whose wings develop externally in the course of a series of larval moults, and (*b*) the Endopterygota, regarded as more advanced in evolution and development, whose wings grow internally and become visible only after the larva has pupated in a cocoon. Of the 21 orders of insects, eight are of freshwater interest: (*a*) Exopterygota: dragonflies and damselflies (order Odonata), stoneflies (order Plecoptera), mayflies (order Ephemeroptera) and true bugs (order Hemiptera); (*b*) Endopterygota: alder flies (order Neuroptera), caddis flies (order Trichoptera), true two-winged flies (order Diptera) and beetles (order Coleoptera).

Aquatic larvae of insects are usually known as nymphs. They are important items in the diet of fish, but fish will also take adult insects if they can get them, including the penultimate stage of maturity in mayflies that anglers call a 'dun' and entomologists a 'sub-imago'. Anglers employ fur, feathers, wire and coloured silk thread to make imitations of all stages as lures for fish. Artificial flies are presented under water or floating on the surface as may be appropriate.

Freshwater Ecology

The Bristol Avon and its tributaries hold only a few species of stoneflies, which are generally intolerant of slow water and summertime fluctuations in dissolved oxygen. Mayflies are less exclusive, however, and there are nearly a score of species represented here in good numbers. Nymphs of the large dark olive spinner (*Baëtis rhodani*) in particular, though preferring strongly flowing water, are tolerant of occasional low oxygen levels; and nymphs of the greendrake mayflies (*Ephemera danica* and *E. vulgata*) are quite at home burrowing into the mud with which much of the river channels becomes lined. Caddis or sedge flies and their larvae are generally plentiful both in species and numbers.

In anticipating and recognizing what mayflies may be on a certain stretch of water it is useful to consider the life-styles of their aquatic nymphs. (*a*) The stone-clinging nymphs, such as *Ecdyonurus* and *Rhithrogena* species, are so structured that they can grip the surface of stones in fast water; the greater the current, the tighter they are forced on to their holdfasts. (*b*) Strongly swimming nymphs, such as *Baëtis* species, are stream-lined and well equipped for holding station in moving water. (*c*) *Ephemerella* nymphs are so structured that while good at swimming they can also penetrate among the tangled roots of weeds and into water moss and accumulated trash. (*d*) *Cloëon* nymphs also have this facility, but exercise it among weeds in slow or still water, being equipped with large gill-plates to assist the uptake of dissolved oxygen, long antennae for exploration and powerful legs for climbing among plant fronds. (*e*) Bottom-crawling nymphs, such as *Paraleptophlebia* and *Caenis* species, are comparatively poor swimmers, whether in moving or still water. (*f*) Burrowing nymphs, such as *Ephemera* species, found in still water, tunnel into silt, for which they are equipped with tusk-like jaws and strong forelegs, their gills being plume-like for optimum oxygen uptake in confined conditions where there is little water movement.

The speed of the water is an important factor, and as may be expected there is some correlation between types of nymph and the habitat zones described in Chapter 2, but in the Bristol Avon catchment the correlation is by no means absolute. The reason for this probably lies in the influence of weirs: between weirs there is an irregularity of river bed that gives both fast and slow water, and at the weirs there are microhabitats, from static to torrential, suiting all types of nymph.

In what follows, an attempt has been made to indicate which flies imitated by anglers have been identified in the Bristol Avon catchment, but the lists are not exhaustive, nor can it be assumed that a specific fly found in a given locality at one time will be found there always. Pollution and the use of pesticides have been blamed for much of this, but there can be little doubt that natural occurrences such as floods, droughts and cold summers also play their parts.

Stoneflies

Adult stoneflies may be recognized by their four narrow, hard and shiny wings, which are laid flat when at rest; most stoneflies have two 'tails' (cerci) but some have only two stumps. The life-cycle is as follows. (*a*) Eggs are dropped by a mated female flying over water; (*b*) wriggling aquatic nymphs ('creepers') hatch out, each with two 'tails', ten abdominal segments and stout double claws on the feet; they take a year to pass through up to 33 moults until (*c*) wings develop, the mature nymph crawls out of the water on to land, inflates its body, casts it last skin and takes to the air. The following species may be recognized locally.

Family	Species	Anglers' name
Perlidae	*Isoperla grammatica*	Yellow Sally
Taeniopterygidae	*Taeniopteryx nebulosa*	February red
Leuctridae	*Leuctra moselyi*	Needle brown
Nemouridae	*Nemoura variegata*	Early brown
Nemouridae	*Amphinemura* species	

Mayflies

Adult mayflies are usually encountered flitting up and down in swarms. They have two large fore-wings, held upright when at rest, and usually two smaller hind-wings (in *Baëtis* very small but in *Caenis* and *Cloëon* entirely absent); usually they have three 'tails' (but in *Baëtis*, *Cloëon*, *Rhithrogena* and *Ecdyonurus* the central 'tail' is vestigial or missing). Mating takes place in the air, and (*a*) mated females deposit eggs on the water surface or attached to under-water objects. (*b*) Tiny aquatic nymphs with three 'tails' hatch out and grow by moulting up to 27 times, over a period of 1-3 years according to species. (*c*) When nearing maturity the nymph undergoes a final moult under water, struggles through the water surface, sometimes by way of emergent vegetation, erects its wings and inflates its body, becoming a sub-imago, called a dun by anglers; its body is dull because of velvet-like hairs over its surface. Then (*d*) the dun's outer skin splits down the back and the shining perfect insect or imago wriggles out – the anglers' 'spinner'. A male is recognizable by having larger and brighter eyes and a pair of claspers associated with the ninth abdominal segment. After mating and egg-laying, spinners die and many of them float on the water surface; these 'spents' are much sought after by rising fish.

Ephemeridae	*Ephemera danica*	Dun, green drake; male spinner, black drake; female spinner, grey drake
Ephemeridae	*Ephemera vulgata*	Dun, green drake; spinners, the mayfly; spents, spent gnat
Leptophlebiidae	*Paraleptophlebia cincta*	Purple dun; purple spinner
Leptophlebiidae	*Habrophlebia fusca*	
Ephemerellidae	*Ephemerella ignita*	Blue-winged olive dun; sherry spinner
Caenidae	*Caenis moesta*	Anglers' curse
Caenidae	*Caenis horaria*	Little white curse
Baëtidae	*Baëtis tenax*	Medium olive dun; medium olive spinner
Baëtidae	*Baëtis rhodani*	Large dark olive dun; large dark olive spinner (male), red spinner (female)
Baëtidae	*Baëtis pumilus*	Iron-blue dun; Jenny spinner (male), little claret spinner (female)
Baëtidae	*Cloëon dipterum*	Pond olive dun; pond olive spinner
Baëtidae	*Cloëon simile*	Lake olive dun; lake olive spinner
Ecdyonuridae	*Rhithrogena semicolorata*	Olive upright dun; yellow upright spinner
Ecdyonuridae	*Rhithrogena germanica*	March brown dun; March brown spinner
Ecdyonuridae	*Ecdyonurus venosus*	Late March brown dun; great red spinner

100

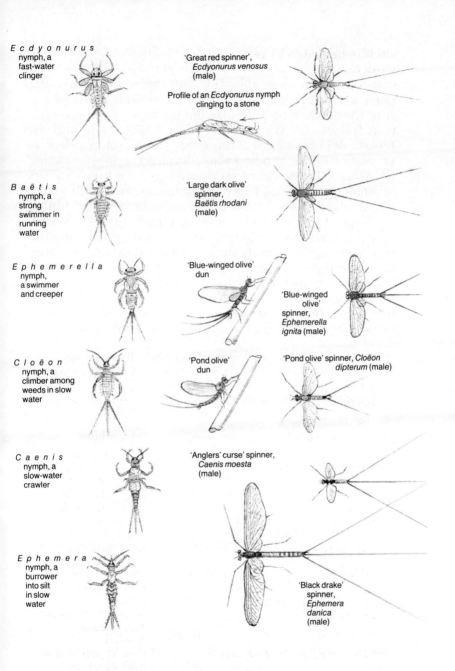

Ecdyonurus nymph, a fast-water clinger

'Great red spinner', Ecdyonurus venosus (male)

Profile of an Ecdyonurus nymph clinging to a stone

Baëtis nymph, a strong swimmer in running water

'Large dark olive' spinner, Baëtis rhodani (male)

Ephemerella nymph, a swimmer and creeper

'Blue-winged olive' dun

'Blue-winged olive' spinner, Ephemerella ignita (male)

Cloëon nymph, a climber among weeds in slow water

'Pond olive' dun

'Pond olive' spinner, Cloëon dipterum (male)

Caenis nymph, a slow-water crawler

'Anglers' curse' spinner, Caenis moesta (male)

Ephemera nymph, a burrower into silt in slow water

'Black drake' spinner, Ephemera danica (male)

Fig. 40 Some mayfly nymphs, duns and spinners

101

Caddis or Sedge Flies

Adult caddis flies, called 'sedges' by anglers, have two pairs of velvety brown wings, held roof-fashion when at rest; they have long antennae but no 'tails'. Their life-cycle is as follows. (a) Mating takes place when at rest and the female deposits eggs on the water surface or attached to vegetation above or below water-level, according to species. (b) Aquatic larvae hatch from the eggs, feed on a variety of small vegetable and animal organisms, and build a shelter of silken webs, in some species elaborated by adding particles of grit or river debris to form a tube – the well-known caddis cases. (c) When well grown the caddis pupates by cocooning itself in its shelter, where it may overwinter. (d) When the pupa has fully undergone its metamorphosis it has strong jaws to tear itself out of its cocoon; it swims to the water surface, penetrates through the surface film into the air (in some species aided by emergent vegetation), rests awhile, then takes to the air as an adult caddis fly.

Rhyacophilidae	*Rhyacophila dorsalis*	Brown sedge
Phryganeidae	*Phryganea grandis*	Great red sedge
Limnephilidae	*Limnephilus lunatus*	Cinnamon sedge
Limnephilidae	*Stenophylax stellatus*	Large cinnamon sedge
Sericostomatidae	*Goëra pilosa*	
Sericostomatidae	*Brachycentrus subnubilis*	Grannom
Leptoceridae	*Leptocerus albifrons*	Silverhorn
Leptoceridae	*Leptocerus cinereus*	Grey silverhorn
Leptoceridae	*Mystacides azurea*	Black silverhorn
Leptoceridae	*Mystacides longicornis*	Brown silverhorn or grouse-wing
Hydropsychidae	*Hydropsyche angustipennis*	Grey sedge
Psychomyidae	*Tinodes waeneri*	Small red sedge
Hydroptilidae	*Hydroptila* species	Little sedge

True Two-winged Flies

What to an entomologist is a true fly has two shiny wings, laid flat when at rest. The life-cycle runs: egg, larva (maggot), resting pupa (chrysalis), adult fly. Anglers' maggots are typical of this order. Many non-aquatic larvae become food for fish by falling from trees. Only a small fraction of the innumerable Diptera species have larvae that live in water, of which the following are typical.

| Simuliidae | *Simulium* species | Black-fly, reed smut |
| Chironomidae | *Chironomus* species | Larva, bloodworm; adult, green midge, olive midge, Blagdon buzzer |

Alder Flies

Adult alder flies have two pairs of shiny dark-brown wings which are held like a coupled roof when at rest. In their life-cycle, (*a*) eggs are laid in waterside vegetation; (*b*) larvae hatching out migrate to slow-moving water, where they live on other insect larvae; (*c*) they then crawl to and pupate in land above water-level, whence (*d*) they eventually emerge as adult flies frequenting the waterside.

| Sialidae | *Sialis lutaria* | Alder fly |

18. Organizations

The Salmon Fishery Act of 1861 was the first of its kind, intended to protect fish stocks as distinct from rights of ownership. Amending and consolidating Acts followed, directed against destructive methods of fishing and obstructions to the passage of migratory fish and against river pollution. Under the Salmon Fisheries Act of 1865 the catchments of the Avon, Brue and Parrett were made a Fishery District with a Board of Conservators based on Bridgwater. The Freshwater Fisheries Act of 1878 (piloted through Parliament, at the request of his 'cloth-capped' constituents, by Mr. A. J. Mundella, M.P. for Sheffield, and known thereafter as the Mundella Act) for the first time gave some protection to the lives of 'coarse' freshwater fish. The Avon, Brue & Parret Fishery Board made fishery byelaws and levied licence duties on fishing rods and other instruments, but its income therefrom was never enough to carry out all its duties effectively over its large district.

The River Avon (Bristol) Catchment Board was set up under the Land Drainage Act of 1930 to remedy some of the abuse and neglect of rivers, specifically to ameliorate flooding on the Bristol Avon and parts of its tributaries scheduled by the Ministry of Agriculture & Fisheries as 'main river'. The war of 1939-45 retarded its progress, but good work was done in clearing the river of fallen trees, obstructive pipe crossings and other bottlenecks.

Then the River Boards Act of 1948 opened a new chapter in river administration. Under its provision the Bristol Avon River Board was set up in 1950 to take over the functions of the Catchment Board and the Fishery Board and the pollution-prevention powers previously held by the county councils and local sanitary authorities. Its income was assured by precepts on the rates of the counties of Gloucestershire, Somerset and Wiltshire and the county boroughs of Bristol and Bath, who delegated representatives. New pollution-prevention Acts of 1951, 1960 and 1961 progressively strengthened its powers for abating pollution.

Under the Water Resources Act of 1963, the Bristol Avon River Board in 1965 became the Bristol Avon River

Authority and took on new tasks of measuring and conserving natural water resources and licensing abstractions both from surface and underground sources. The principle of unified river-basin management was advanced still further by the Water Act of 1973, which set up ten regional all-purpose water authorities for all of England and Wales.

The Wessex Water Authority thus came into office on 1st April 1974 to carry out duties in the fields of water supply, sewerage and sewage disposal, land drainage, water pollution prevention, freshwater fisheries conservation, water-based recreation, and amenity, previously the responsibility of water boards, local sanitary authorities and the river authorities for the Bristol Avon, the Somerset rivers and the Salisbury Avon and Dorset rivers. It consists of representatives of county and district councils together with government appointees nominated by the Department of the Environment and the Ministry of Agriculture, Fisheries & Food, one of the latter expressly to represent fishery interests. It operates in three divisions based on the earlier river authority areas, each division having a local committee structure representing district councils, the Sports Council, the Country Landowners' Association, the National Farmers' Union, the Confederation of British Industry and local fisheries advisory committees, the latter widely drawn to represent all aspects of fishing. Income is derived mainly from charges for water supply, sewerage and sewage disposal, and from precepts on the county councils and government grants, but a small part comes from fishing licences. Fishing law has been updated by the Salmon & Freshwater Fisheries Act of 1975, under which fishery byelaws have been made, dealing with close seasons, prohibited instruments for taking fish, unlawful removal of fish, minimum sizes and maximum numbers of fish allowed to be taken, and other details designed to protect fish stocks. Copies of the byelaws and the scales of licence duties may be obtained from the Divisional Fisheries & Recreations Officer, Wessex Water Authority, P.O. Box 95, Quay House, The Ambury, Bath, BA1 2YP.

A notable feature of the Bristol Avon is that most of the river banks and the fishing rights that go with them are in private ownership and are leased to small syndicates and organized angling clubs. Land transactions arising from major land drainage schemes have not here enabled the Water Authority to acquire fishing rights over sizeable stretches as has happened in some other catchments.

There is very little 'free and open' water. Between Netham Dam and Hanham Weir, where the Avon was ordinarily tidal until Bristol's Floating Harbour was constructed early in the 19th century, members of the public still have the right of fishing, but access is limited to the towpath or boats. At Bath, the City Council allows angling on the Avon from Pulteney Weir down to Newbridge wherever accessible from public footways, and usage seems to have established free fishing from the footpath on the north side of the river between Bathampton Weir and Fiveways Garage (the top field excepted). North Wiltshire District Council allows free fishing from town land below Chippenham; and it is also allowed at Malmesbury on the Sherston branch of the Avon adjoining the town recreation ground, and on the Tetbury branch between Abbey Weir and the one-time station yard.

The Bristol Waterworks Company offers world-famous fishing on some of its reservoirs. One of these, Chew Valley Lake, was made by damming the River Chew; it is 2¼ miles (3.6 km) long and has a water perimeter of 10 miles (16 km). It was opened to the public for angling on 1st May 1957, before which it was stocked with 805,000 trout fry and 17,000 trout yearlings, both brown and rainbow, with phenomenal fishing results. Restocking is continued annually from the Company's own hatchery on Blagdon Lake at Ubley, in the next watershed. There is fishing from boats as well as from the banks; part of the water surface is used for sailing, and parts of the waterside are used for picnics and bird-watching. Particulars of permits and charges may be obtained from the Bristol Waterworks Company's Fisheries & Recreations Officer at Woodford Lodge, Chew Stoke, Bristol, BS18 8XH.

Fishing syndicates and clubs in the Bristol Avon catchment number over forty. Most of these are federated to either the Bristol & West of England Federation of Anglers or the North Somerset & West Wilts Federation of Anglers, and through these bodies to the National Federation of Anglers. Their secretaries, addresses, telephone numbers and waters may change from time to time, but up-to-date lists of angling associations and of licence distributors are periodically printed in Wessex Water Authority's fishing publications. Some of the angling associations date back to the days when railways and bicycles first popularized angling excursions. Many of them offer visitors' tickets through their secretaries or local fishing-tackle dealers.

SOME OLD-ESTABLISHED ANGLING CLUBS

> Silver Dace Angling Association, founded 1874
> Avon & Tributaries A.A., 1876
> Bristol Golden Carp A.A., 1879
> City of Bristol A.A., 1880
> Somerfords Fishing Association, 1884
> Bath Anglers' Association, 1895
> Avon Preservation & Restocking Society, 1908
> Knowle (Bristol) Angling Association, 1923
> Portcullis A.A., 1923
> Bristol & District Amalgamated Anglers (incorporating ten, later eleven established associations), 1967

A few private estates allow their waters to be fished by arrangement with their estate offices. Particulars are subject to changes, but some guidance may be found in Appendix 2.

The Bristol Avon Area Fish Records Panel was set up in 1959 and consists of delegates from Wessex Water Authority, the Bristol & West of England Federation of Anglers and the North Somerset & West Wilts Federation of Anglers. It collaborates with the British Record (Rod-caught) Fish Committee. Secretarial services are provided by the Water Authority, with which contact should immediately be made in the event of capture of a specimen fish. There are strict rules for verifying the identity, exact weight and other relevant details of specimens.

19. Fishery Management

Reference has been made earlier to the effect of geology and other local factors upon the character of a river. To sum up, here in the Bristol Avon catchment our rivers and streams are consistently alkaline, rich in calcium and other mineral elements, and fertilized by nitrates and phosphates from effluents – all conducive to the growth of plants and invertebrate animals in productivity chains. There are many weirs, which tend to be obstructive to the movement of fish but retain water very usefully in times of low flow. Not so favourable are the clay subsoils: they cause flashy run-off, they erode into deep and often sunless channels, and they make the water cloudy and deposit muds, which smother redds and are unstable media for fine weeds and invertebrate animals. The Kennet & Avon Canal and the older lakes and ponds are eutrophic, and even the lowland river goes eutrophic in summer. The unfavourable factors emphasize a need to make the best possible use of what is available for the food of fish in order to obtain optimum yields of fish.

Objectives

In commercial fisheries there is a clear objective – profit – and the fishing industry is directed accordingly. On the Bristol Avon the objective is recreational fishing, but how best to provide it is not always clear-cut, for the diversity of waters and easy accessibility by motor transport from centres of population attract at least four categories of anglers, each with slightly different requirements.

Match fishermen are numerous, angling with highly sophisticated tackle in competition for the greatest aggregate weights of coarse fish, which are held in keep-nets but put back after final weighing. Any injured fish become food for gulls and herons without serious loss to fish stocks. (Herons are the traditional predators upon freshwater fish, but since the middle of the present century black-headed gulls have become common inland and herring gulls have established themselves on roof tops in towns, living by

scavenging.) Betting adds excitement to fishing competitions, and profitability for the experts. The lowland reaches
of the Bristol Avon are well suited to match fishing. In
August 1975, Mr. Dave Baker caught 78 lb 9 oz 8 drm of
fish (35.650 kg) in a 5 hour competition pegged on the
Avon at Ladydown, near Trowbridge, an average of 15 lb
11 oz 8 drm (7.130 kg) per hour. In June 1977, the same
angler took 50 lb 11 oz (22.991 kg) in a 3 hour competition
on the Avon at Melksham, an hourly average of 16 lb 14
oz 5 drm (7.661 kg). His 5 hour record was broken in 1984
by Mr. Andrew R. Burton, who took 79 lb 8 oz 0 drm
(36.061 kg) on the Avon at Chippenham, an hourly average
of 15 lb 14 oz 6 drm (7.212 kg). In July 1985, these records
were smashed by Mr. Mervyn ('Topper') Haskins, who in
5 hours' fishing on the Avon at Swineford took 114 lb 3
oz 0 drm (51.794 kg) of fish, mostly bream, an hourly
average of 22 lb 13 oz 6 drm (10.359 kg). This was followed
almost immediately by a 5½ hour match record from the
Avon at Chippenham, where Mr. Frank Coe caught 146
lb 9 oz 0 drm (66.480 kg) of bream, an hourly average of
26 lb 10 oz 6 drm (12.087 kg). National championships
have been held on the Avon with highly satisfactory results,
as summarized in Appendix 3.

Game-fishermen are numerous, angling as a rule (a rule
not always observed) with artificial flies for trout, which
on most occasions are taken home to be cooked for food.
Taking trout for food is a healthy natural instinct; a trout
that has been hooked would have a poor chance of survival
if returned to the water, and on lakes inclined to go eutrophic, taking fish away helps to reduce unwanted fertility;
but the practice can seriously deplete trout stocks unless
something positive is done to make good the losses.

Next come the specimen-hunters, often out early or late
in the day, who concentrate their skills on outstandingly
large fish, especially pike, carp or barbel. And fourth but by
no means least come the general anglers, true followers of
Isaak Walton, solitary or in small parties, fishing with various
baits for various fish, relaxing in the open air and enjoying
the diversion from everyday cares that fishing offers.

Fortunately the diverse requirements of anglers are to
some extent met by differences in habitat zones and the fish
they hold, but good management has to recognize and recon-

cile any outstanding differences. Regard must also be paid to other forms of water-based recreation, to amenity, and to the needs of public health, water supply, land drainage, industry and agriculture. Occasionally it is necessary to take steps to ensure that events do not conflict, and as activities tend to increase, such occasions may become frequent.

Food: a Fundamental

At one time it was assumed that fishing would always be improved by planting more fish: it was argued that they would not only add to present numbers but would breed with existing stocks and develop hybrid vigour and larger specimens. If the fish planted were a different species it was assumed they would add variety to the fishing.

An investigation by the Freshwater Biological Association, started before and completed after the Second World War, showed that (granted a sufficiency of clean water containing dissolved oxygen and free of poisons) the foundation of fish growth is food. Each species has its preferred foods, which may vary according to the age of a fish, but if the preferred foods are in short supply fish can accommodate themselves to alternatives. If a fish has insufficient food it will be stunted, but given sufficient food even a stunted fish will start to grow well and will continue to grow practically throughout its life.

The best use of available natural foods is achieved where there are several sorts of fish, so that different species each seek out their preferences and leave scarcely any kind of food unused. This applies particularly to coarse fish in the lowland river, where there is a wide spread of both carnivorous and herbivorous appetites. In the hill streams there is something to be said for encouraging grayling alongside trout, for similar reasons. Snobbery dies hard, but grayling are a delight to eat and could relieve the pressure on trout taken for the table.

The vast numbers of eggs that coarse fish produce are evidence of their ability to perpetuate themselves while leaving ample margins for predation and any other natural disasters. When fish in an established fishery are smaller than similar species elsewhere, the probability is that there are too many mouths chasing too little food. To plant more fish in such circumstances would aggravate food shortage, and an improvement might be achieved by reducing the numbers of fish.

Restocking: Coarse Fish

The need for restocking arises when there are man-made disasters such as fatal pollution or over-fishing. Restocking falls into two categories: coarse fish and trout. In the Bristol Avon catchment, needs in the first category have usually been met by finding other waters that are over-stocked or about to be drained; the second category demands hatchery-raised fish.

A classic example of restocking with coarse fish occurred soon after the Second World War. In the 'Baedeker' air raids on Bath on 25th and 26th April 1942, the gas works and public sewers were smashed and foul liquids escaped to the Avon, killing off fish practically all the way to Bristol. As soon as post-war conditions allowed, the Avon Preservation & Restocking Society used its equipment and expertise to help local angling associations restock their sections of river. Many of the roach transplanted were portly specimens netted from the lake at Fonthill Bishop, forty miles away. The A.P.R.S. is a body of volunteers whose purpose is to protect and improve the fishing of the Bristol Avon and its tributaries, and in particular to rescue fish in danger and to restock after any loss by pollution. Another memorable operation was the netting of Duchess Pond, near Stapleton, when it was about to be filled in, whereby hundreds of large carp, including mirror carp up to 22½ lb (10 kg) in weight, were salvaged and transferred to other local waters. In yet another operation a thousand common bream, each around the 2 lb (1 kg) size, were rescued from the Golden Valley Mill pond at Bitton. Not all such activities, which have sometimes numbered a dozen sorties in a year, give spectacular results, but over the years the A.P.R.S. has usefully transplanted many hundreds of thousands of fish.

Parts of the Kennet & Avon Canal are subject to leakage because of slipping hillsides. Whenever leaks have occurred it has been necessary to isolate a section of canal with stopboards and drain it out in order to pug the bottom with clay. It is possible to let fish go with the water through hatches to the river below, but inevitably this leaves fish stranded and a salvage operation is called for. When the two mile (3.2 km) pound from Limpley Stoke to Avoncliff was drained out in 1953, it was first swept by net for its whole length; a grass-snake, disturbed at Limpley Stoke, swam in front of the net all the way to Avoncliff Aqueduct.

To meet the probability of having to restock after pollution incidents the Wessex Water Authority now has stock ponds of roach, bream, carp and tench at its major sewage works; besides being available to transplant at short notice, these fish are indicators of effective treatment of the effluent with which the ponds are kept filled.

Sweep-nets are now supplemented by electrical apparatus. Electrical culling was first used in the Bristol Avon catchment area in 1953, when portable generators improvised by Mr. W. Gilbert Hartley of the M.A.F.F. Salmon & Freshwater Fisheries Department and Lt.-Col. B. E. Hammond-Davies of the Piscatorial Society were used to seek and remove coarse fish in the catchment of Chew Valley Lake, then under construction. At the conclusion of the operation its effectiveness was proved by testing with rotenone, a narcotic, the water being temporarily impounded by the new dam. The reappearance of roach in Chew Valley Lake a few years later has not been satisfactorily explained: was it due to carriage of spawn on the feet of birds, or illicit use of live-bait or deliberate planting inspired by malice?

Following the use of electrical fishing in the Chew valley and some experiments of its own, the Bristol Avon River Board in 1957 invested in a 1.5 kVA alternating-current generator giving 230 volts at 50 cycles per second; this was supplemented by a metal rectifier and a large choke so that either alternating or direct current could be used. Local waters have an electrical conductivity of about 750 dionic units (microsiemens) per centimetre cube, which is more than that of soft moorland waters but less than that of sea water or of fish blood lymph, so is in a range suitable for electrical fishing. The apparatus has proved effective for culling and census-taking on small rivers and streams, but in wide and deep rivers and lakes it is not far-reaching, so fish can avoid its field unless restricted by stop-nets.

Further experiment has shown the value of pulsed direct current, fish being attracted to the positive electrode.

Restocking: Trout

Once upon a time, when people with leisure were few, wild trout in England could reproduce and survive in sufficient numbers to maintain their species in spite of natural losses. A growing threat from humanity was recognized in 19th century legislation (the Salmon Fisheries Act of 1873) which granted brown trout an annual close season. Trout fishing in the rivers and streams of the Bristol Avon river system is today so popular that a young trout has a very poor chance of surviving to the age of four years or so, when it would be mature enough to spawn, and the progeny even of a surviving pair face many hazards.

When, in 1950, the newly formed Bristol Avon River Board took over freshwater fisheries administration from the Avon, Brue & Parret Fishery Board, a high priority was given to eliminating poisonous discharges and reducing the biochemical oxygen demands of effluents, but early recognition was given to the problem of maintaining and supplementing trout stocks at a cost commensurate with income from trout rod licences, then only about £500 per annum. In the winter of 1950-51, some Vibert boxes, small perforated plastic containers, were filled with fertile trout eggs and buried in apparently clean gravels of the River Chew near Chew Magna and the Lam Brook at Woolley, to simulate redds. A few weeks later it was found that all the eggs had died, having been suffocated by mud; clearly this was not a method suitable for local waters. In the next two years some thousands of brown-trout alevins, surplus to the needs of Bristol Waterworks Company's fisheries, were liberated into selected hill streams, but with no observable benefit. Experimental plantings of several thousand fingerling brown trout were made each springtime from 1953 to 1961. These fish were hatchery-reared, from 4 to 8 inches (10-20 cm) in length, and in the first five years were identified by clipping the tip of a pectoral, pelvic or adipose fin, a different fin each year; but in spite of wide publicity through angling associations and licence distributors the numbers of adult trout with a clipped fin reported captured were negligible. It was concluded from this and other evidence that the survival rate of young trout in our streams is not good, the reasons probably being predation (by water birds, fish, dragonfly larvae, boys and others) and a deficiency of fine weeds in which small fish and their food organisms can take shelter.

During the 1950s, the River Board also collaborated with angling associations in marking rainbow trout of takeable size with numbered gill-tags and planting in various locations. It was found that rainbow trout are so vigorous that they readily tear off gill-tags (better methods of marking have since been developed), but sufficient tagged fish were recovered to confirm that rainbow trout wander widely, and that fishing pressure on trout stocks is such that a large proportion of fish will be recaptured soon after being planted.

It was finally concluded that the demand for takeable trout can best be met by planting out well-fed hatchery-reared trout, aged at least fifteen months, at intervals just before and during the trout-fishing season, a policy adopted by the River Board in 1962 and continued by the River Authority (1965-74) and its successor, the Wessex Water Authority.

In June 1965, two thousand 7-inch (18 cm) hatchery-reared brown trout were liberated without ceremony into the Bristol Frome, where the newly completed Frome Valley trunk sewer had ended half a century of river pollution. In the following years, when it became certain that the Bristol Frome was once again a trout river, consignments of larger brown trout were allocated to the Frome as part of the general programme, and local angling organizations joyfully added trout from their own resources.

The cost of trout licences has increased more than can be attributed to inflation. There can be little doubt, however, that the trout angler gets far better value for his money today.

New Species

In the second half of the 19th century, when railways and steamboats had popularized the transport of passengers and goods, it became a fashion to introduce new species of plants and animals into places far from their origins. In 1864, some European catfish or wels (*Silurus glanis*) were brought to Britain from eastern Europe; ugly though they were, they aroused interest and more were imported and planted into English waters. A story is told that the Marquess of Bath acquired some in 1872 and liberated them into the lakes at Longleat, but three years later he had the lakes drained to get rid of them because they had eaten all the trout there. The story carries a warning for our own time.

In introducing a new species there is a risk that it might compete with or dominate similar species, that it might prove undesirably predatory, or that it might increase unpredictably, to the detriment of other considerations. Bleak probably got into the Bristol Avon as escaped live-bait brought from the Thames; they have invoked many a curse because they come in shoals to nibble and disturb baits intended for larger species.

The introduction of common bream into the Bristol Avon might have proved disastrous because it was not known at the time to what extent bream compete with the native roach. Indeed some anglers maintain that Bristol Avon roach are no longer what they used to be and bream are the reason. Certainly there seem to be no specimen roach nowadays; the record for a local roach, 2 lb 12 oz (1.247 kg), dates back as far as 1948 and relates to water (Chew Magna Reservoir) where there are no bream. If bream now dominate roach in the lowland river, this is what competition anglers want, but common sense dictates that bream should be confined to waters that are fished in competitions and not allowed to spread into the hill streams.

Bleak, common bream and barbel are not native to the Bristol Avon nor generally to other rivers of western England. Why, then, are they found naturally in the rivers of eastern England? An explanation might be found in events during and following the Great Ice Age, which ended some 10,000 years ago. Although there is little evidence to suggest that what is now the Bristol Avon was actually submerged under glaciers, its waters for long and repeated periods consisted largely of ice melt, which would have been too cold for these species to spawn and reproduce

115

in. The same events overwhelmed eastern England, but rivers there were later able to replenish their stocks of fish from Continental rivers, with which they were connected until Britain was finally cut off by sea from the rest of Europe when sinking land surfaces opened the Strait of Dover and allowed the North Sea to transgress into the English Channel. The artificial introduction of barbel from waters in the Thames catchment in 1955 and 1964-71 has added a species highly valued by anglers for its sporting qualities; the waters of the Bristol Avon and its larger tributaries warm up just sufficiently in the month of May to permit successful natural spawning and incubation of eggs.

Apart from suitability or otherwise of new species, the planting of live fish from uncertified sources carries risks of introducing new fish diseases or reinforcing existing endemics. The same is true of planting fish foods from uncertain sources, particularly freshwater snails and crustaceans, which are intermediate hosts for flukes and tapeworms. The importation of live fish from abroad may now be done only under licence from the Ministry of Agriculture, Fisheries & Food. Section 30 of the Salmon & Freshwater Fisheries Act of 1975 forbids the planting of fish or fish spawn into inland waters without the Water Authority's specific written consent.

Neglected Waters

The Water Authority exercises a power under the Land Drainage Act to cut down or trim obstructive trees that might aggravate flooding, but this power is confined to the rivers and streams that have been scheduled by the Ministry of Agriculture as 'main river', and it cannot be exercised merely to clear swims or let in light, nor on the unscheduled minor watercourses. There are many miles of hill stream that are practically unfished but could be made fishable by devoted attention from riparian owners or their lessees. Shaded, deep-channelled, small streams need to have the trees on their southern banks reduced to a minimum in order to admit light. The trunks should be cut flush with the bank, not left sticking up like a sore thumb, and the banks should continue to receive attention

116

in the following years for removal of aftergrowth. Light having been admitted to the channel, pieces of crowfoot can be dibbled into the stream bed and pieces of watercress at the margins – rather like planting out cabbage seedlings or, more appropriately, rice under water in a paddy field.

Such streams might also be improved by low fishing weirs, which will create holding pools, bring the water surface nearer to the sunlight and smooth out some of the flashy nature of wet-weather flows. Fishing weirs require the prior consent of the Water Authority, whose staff can offer useful advice on the manner of construction. Whether built of stone, concrete blocks or timber, it is important that the sides of a weir should extend well into the bank on each side and that the foot of the weir should be substantially paved to prevent scour and undercutting of the foundation, which would lead to collapse.

Local geology may have shaped our river's character, but it is sunlight, working through the productivity patterns of plants and animals, that gives the river life.

Appendix 1

IDENTIFICATION OF FISH
IN THE BRISTOL AVON CATCHMENT

By working through the following chart from the beginning it should be possible to identify any fish present naturally in the Bristol Avon catchment, but the numbered side headings should also make it possible to pick up the threads at any stage of identification.

1 Shape
Flattened; both eyes on upper side of body : Flounder; see p. 95
Snake-like → 2
More or less torpedo-shaped → 3

2 Mouth
Round, sucker-like : Lamprey; see p. 31
Very large and long, bristling with sharp teeth on tongue and both jaws : Pike; see p. 53
More or less ordinary → 3

3 Fins
No pectoral or ventral fins : Lamprey → 2
No ventral fins but one long dorsal fin : Eel; see p. 55
Two pectoral and two ventral fins, but only one dorsal fin, placed about the middle of the back → 4
Ditto, but with one dorsal fin placed near the tail, more or less over the anal fin → 5
Two pectoral and two ventral fins, and two dorsal fins → 6

4 Only one dorsal fin, on middle of back
Mouth small and toothless (teeth being in the throat); lateral line obvious (except possibly on minnow) : Carp family and Loach → 9
Mouth with very small teeth; no lateral line : Shad; see p. 51

5 Only one dorsal fin, placed near tail
No spines; large snout : Pike; see p. 53
Three spines in front of dorsal fin : Stickleback; see p. 93

6 Two dorsal fins
One rayed fin in middle of back and a very small rayless (adipose) fin nearer tail : Salmon family → 7

Long gap between dorsal fins; anterior fin short, with four spines; posterior also short but with soft rays; no lateral line; estuarine : Grey mullet; see p. 90

Dorsal fins close together or continuous, anterior spiny, posterior shorter than anterior and with soft rays : Perch family → 8

Dorsal fins close together, anterior spiny and short (6-9 spines), posterior soft-rayed (15-19 rays) and three times as long; large spiny pectoral fins; a small fish with large head : Bullhead; see p. 91

7 Salmon family: all have a little adipose fin on back near tail

Large dorsal fin (4-7 hard rays and 13-17 branched rays) with stripes of dark and iridescent colouring : Grayling; see p. 49

Dorsal fin has 3-5 hard rays and 10-12 (rarely 9) branched rays; tail fin slightly forked or concave : Salmon; see p. 39

Dorsal fin has 3 hard rays and 8-10 (rarely 11) branched rays; end of tail fin nearly straight : Trout; see pp. 39,45

8 Perch family

Dorsal fins continuous, anterior 11-16 hard spines, posterior 11-15 soft rays; body speckled; iris mauve : Ruff; see p. 88

Dorsal fins not continuous, anterior with 9 hard spines, posterior with smaller spines and 11 soft rays; body slim and silvery; estuarine : Bass; see p. 89

Dorsal fins not continuous, the anterior longer (13-17 spines) than the posterior (1-2 hard and 13-15 soft rays); body deep; five or more vertical dark stripes on yellowish sides and a black spot at rear end of anterior dorsal fin; iris of eye golden : Perch; see p. 87

9 Carp family and Loach; only one dorsal fin; pectoral fins placed rather low beneath shoulder; ventral fins located at mid-belly; anal fin and tail fin well developed; lateral line present (incomplete in minnow, indistinct in loach); mouth toothless (teeth back in throat)

Tail fin not forked, forming a single lobe; barbels six : Loach; see p. 84

Tail fin wide, tending to form two lobes; barbels four (rarely more), two or nil: Carp family → 10

10 Carp family

Dorsal fin long (including 14-23 branched rays) but anal fin short (13 or less branched rays) : Carp and Goldfish → 11

Dorsal fin short (13 or less branched rays) and anal fin short (13 or less branched rays) → 13

Dorsal fin short (13 or less branched rays) but anal fin long (15-30 branched rays) : Bream and Bleak → 18

119

11 *Carp and Goldfish*
Four small barbels : Common carp; see p. 61
No barbels : genus *Carassius* →12

12 *Genus Carassius*
Edge of dorsal fin slightly rounded; scales in lateral line 28-35; scales between lateral line and leading edge of dorsal fin 6½-9 : Crucian carp; see p. 64
Dorsal fin slightly angular, with strong spine at leading edge; scales in lateral line 25-30; scales between lateral line and leading edge of dorsal fin 5-6½ : Goldfish; see p. 64

13 *Short dorsal fin, short anal fin*
Mouth with barbels → 14
No barbels → 15

14 *With barbels*
Barbels four (rarely five or six) : Barbel; see p. 65
Barbels two; mouth terminal, very down-turned; scales small; fins well rounded : Tench; see p. 69
Barbels two; mouth under snout; scales relatively large; fins not rounded : Gudgeon; see p. 67

15 *No barbels*
Scales very small; fish small : Minnow; see p.
Scales relatively large → 16

16 *Scales relatively large*
Edges of dorsal and anal fins slightly rounded; lateral line has 42-49 scales : Chub; see p. 76
Edges of dorsal and anal fins slightly concave → 17

17 *Concave dorsal and anal fins*
Body narrow and shallow; fins yellowish grey, dorsal with 3 hard and 7-8 soft rays, anal 3 hard and 7-9 soft rays; lateral line has 47-54 scales (rarely 45-55) : Dace; see p. 75
Body well proportioned; iris of eye crimson; fins orange (especially ventrals and tail, others greyer); dorsal fin poised midway between snout and root of tail, immediately over ventrals; dorsal and anal fins each have 3 hard and 9-12 soft rays; lateral line 40-46 scales (rarely 38-47) : Roach; see p. 71
Body fairly deep; iris of eye yellow; ventral, anal and tail fins bright red; dorsal fin placed behind midway point, noticeably posterior to ventrals; dorsal fin has 2-3 hard and 8-9 soft rays, anal fin 3 hard and 9-12 soft rays; lateral line has 39-44 scales (rarely 38-44) : Rudd; see p. 74
Body slim but well proportioned; tissues suffused with pink; dorsal fin has 3 hard and 8-9 soft rays, anal 3 hard and 9-11 soft rays; lateral line has 56-61 scales : Golden orfe; see p. 78

18 Bream and Bleak; abdomen forms sharp edge not spanned by scales
> Body slim : Bleak; see p. 81
> Body narrow but deep; dorsal fin has 3 hard and 9 (rarely 8-10) soft rays; anal fin is deep, with 3 hard and 23-30 soft rays; lateral line has 51-56 scales (rarely 49-60) : Common or bronze bream; see p. 78
> Body very narrow but deep; dorsal fin has 3 hard and 8-9 soft rays; anal fin, 3 hard and 19-24 soft rays; lateral line has 43-51 scales : Silver bream; see pp. 78,80

Hybrids between members of the carp family are not uncommon; they have characteristics that are intermediate between those of the parents.

Difficult cases of identification may be referred to the Divisional Fisheries & Recreations Officer of the Wessex Water Authority (Quay House, The Ambury, Bath, BA1 2YP), who can authorize removal of fish from the water in which captured and if necessary arrange transport or refrigeration. A fish can then be sent on either to the Wessex Water Authority's Regional Biologist at Poole, Dorset, or to the Keeper of Zoology (Fisheries Section), British Museum (Natural History), Cromwell Road, London, SW7 5BD (telephone 01 589 6323).

Appendix 2

FISHABLE WATERS
OTHER THAN THE RIVER

Badminton Park Lake (Beaufort Estate Office, Badminton, Glos.): carp.

Barrow Reservoirs (Fisheries & Recreations Officer, Bristol Waterworks Company, Woodford Lodge, Chew Stoke, Bristol, BS18 8XH): brown and rainbow trout.

Berkeley Lake, near Frome (Frome & District A.A.): roach, tench, bream.

Bitterwell Lake, near Bristol (Mrs. S. Scully, The Chalet, Bitterwell Lake, Coalpit Heath, Bristol): carp and other coarse fish.

Bowood Lake, Calne (Estate Office, Bowood, Calne, Wilts.): roach, tench, bream, perch, pike.

Braydon Pond, near Malmesbury: trout, pike.

Breech Valley Trout Fishery (Mrs. M. Harris, Tweed Farm, Coleford, Bath): trout.

Bristol Floating Harbour and Feeder Canal (Bristol City Council, lessee Bristol City Docks A.C.): roach, bream, eel, carp, tench, pike, perch, flounder, dace, minnow; a few rudd and occasional but rare trout and sea trout.

Cameley Trout Lakes, Temple Cloud (J. Harris, Hillcrest Farm, Cameley, Temple Cloud, Bristol); special facilities for the disabled: trout.

Chew Magna Reservoir (Bristol Waterworks Company; see Chew Valley Lake): roach, trout.

Chew Valley Lake (Fisheries & Recreations Officer, Bristol Waterworks Company, Woodford Lodge, Chew Stoke, Bristol, BS18 8XH): brown and rainbow trout, eel, roach, perch.

Dunkirk Pond, near Devizes (E. F. Giles, Lakeside, Rowde, Devizes, Wilts.): roach, carp, tench.

Eastville Lake, Bristol (Bristol City Council, Parks Department, Cabot House, Deanery Road, Bristol): roach and other coarse fish.

Emborough Pond – see Lechmere.

Erlestoke Lake, near Devizes (Lavington Angling Club): roach and other coarse fish.

Ham Green Lake, Pill (Bristol & Weston Health Authority, Ham Green Hospital): roach, carp, tench, perch.

Henleaze Lake, near Westbury-on-Trym (Warden, Mr. D. F. Klemperer, 25 Rockside Drive, Henleaze, Bristol): roach, perch, carp, tench, rainbow trout.

Hunstrete Lake, near Marksbury (Bathampton A.A.): roach, tench, carp, bream, eel.

Kennet & Avon Canal (Devizes Angling Association, Bradford-on-Avon & District A.A., Bristol & West of England Federation of Anglers, Bathampton A.A.): roach, tench, carp, bream, pike, eel, perch, rudd, minnow, gudgeon, crucian carp.

Lechmere, also called Emborough Pond (limited day tickets from Water Keeper or from Thatcher's Tackle, 18 Queen Street, Wells, Somerset): roach, tench, crucian carp, perch.

Longleat Lakes (The Agent, Longleat House, Warminster, Wilts; Water Keeper Mr. P. Bundy, Parkhill Cottage, Longleat): roach and other coarse fish.

Marston Lake, near Frome: roach, carp, tench, rudd, pike.

Orchardleigh Lake (Frome & District A.A.; no day tickets): roach, perch, pike, carp, tench.

St. George's Lake, Bristol (Bristol City Council, Parks Department, Cabot House, Deanery Road, Bristol): roach and other coarse fish.

Silverlands Gravel Pit, Lacock: roach, common carp, tench, perch, crucian carp.

Tucking Mill Lake, Monkton Combe (Wessex W.A., Quay House, The Ambury, Bath, BA1 2YP); special facilities for the disabled: roach and other coarse fish.

Westbury Ponds, Wilts. (Eden Vale A.A., White Horse A.A., Bath A.A.): coarse fish.

Witham Friary Ponds, near Frome: carp, roach, crucian carp.

Woodborough Pond, near Radstock (Bathampton A.A.): carp, tench.

Woodland Park Lake, near Westbury, Wilts. (Woodland Park Estate Office, Brokerswood, Westbury, Wilts.): roach, tench.

Wootton Bassett Lake (Wootton Bassett A.C.): roach and other coarse fish.

N.F.A. CHAMPIONSHIPS
ON THE BRISTOL AVON

A summary from results issued on each occasion by the National Federation of Anglers

	9th September 1972 (1st Division)	9th September 1978 (1st Division)	11th September 1982 (2nd Division)
Associations competing	79	79	74
Competitors	948	948	888
Competitors failing to weigh	68	11	26
Total weight of fish	1659 lb 11½ oz	2103 lb 9½ oz	2375 lb 10¼ oz
Average weight per competitor	1 lb 12 oz	2 lb 3 oz	2 lb 10¾ oz

Section Winners' Weights

Section and vicinity 1972	lb	oz	Section and vicinity 1978	lb	oz	lb	oz
A Willsbridge	8	5½	**A** Somerdale	17	12	11	12
B Bitton	4	7¾	**B** Bitton	8	9	18	13½
C Saltford	4	13½	(The original Saltford section, on both sides of the river, has been divided and allocated to the adjoining sections.)				
D Kelston	2	15	**C** Kelston	9	6	8	4
E Newton St. Loe	6	13	**D** Newton St. Loe	5	4¾	10	4
F Newbridge	3	1½	**E** Newbridge	5	8	17	13
G Batheaston	9	6½	**F** Batheaston	20	12	18	3
H Claverton	33	8	**G** Claverton	10	4	18	6½
J Limpley Stoke	21	12	**H** Limpley Stoke	16	7½	16	3
K Winsley	17	2¾	**J** Winsley	10	15	12	15
L Bradford-on-Avon	22	0	**K** Bradford-on-Avon	10	10	37	9½
M Staverton	9	2½	**L** Staverton	48	13	44	5½
			M Melksham	16	12¼	14	10

Individual Winners' Weights

	1972		1978		1982	
	lb	oz	lb	oz	lb	oz
1st	33	8	48	13	44	5½
2nd	22	0	25	14½	37	9½
3rd	21	12	20	12	18	13½
4th	18	12	17	12	18	7½
5th	17	2¾	16	12¼	18	6½
6th	15	13	16	7½	18	3
7th	14	11½	15	7½	17	13
8th	14	3½	13	8½	17	10
9th	14	0	13	0	16	3
10th	13	15	11	11	15	10½
11th	13	4	10	15	15	8¼
12th	12	12	10	13½	15	8

Index

126

127

128